AF350871

LIGHT OF THE FORCE

A SEEKER'S GUIDE

BY

J. A Mchaels

LIGHT OF THE FORCE
A Seeker's Guide
Copyright © 2023 Jared A. Michaels

ALL RIGHTS RESERVED

ISBN: 979-8-3304-8662-5
Published by: Independent Publication

DEDICATION

I dedicate this book to those who have brought me the most terrible, yet insightful lessons. I have come to learn that it often takes some break in the way we see the world to see what is behind the illusions and delusions that we latch onto so as to make life easy.

I dedicate this book to those who have been there, next to me as I broke, as we all do. We may walk our own Path, but that does not mean that the Force put others next to us to merely watch. We all need a hand once in a while.

I dedicate this to my spiritual traveling companions along the Way:

- **Chris**, who helped me take my first steps into this new world.
- **Joshua**, who helped me to break the arrogance of an angry youth who was no longer too weak to save himself.
- **Charles**, who had been a powerful friend and sounding board for my rantings and growth along the Way.
- **Eric**, who has been a voice of both caution and insight, whose help with the editing of this text was invaluable.

Thank you, all.

Other Works by Author

Jedi Path:

From Nerd to Knight: The Story of a Traveler of the Jedi Way
Feb 2012
ISBN 13: **978-1469999609**
This is the story of one man's quest to find purpose in life, and finding it locked within the boundaries of the fictional warrior-monks, the Jedi. Herein lies a harsh look at the actions, and growth, of a man, from his youth to now, looking to grow beyond the constraints of the world in which he was reared.

The Road I Walk
Jul 2013
ISBN 13: **978-1491021750**
As we progress deeper into the new era of human development, the need for a guiding light becomes greater and greater. This is that guiding light for those who take the Jedi Path as their way of life. This is not the tale of any man, but the spirit of the Jedi Way, as seen by its longest active voice.

Spirit Warrior Series:

Sword of Fire: Lessons for the Spirit Warrior
Feb 2013
ISBN 13: **978-1482369038**
Sword of Fire is the tale of one man on his quest to be a better person, and to understand the workings of the world, all the while making it a better place for those around him. It is the words of a teacher, as he delves into some of the philosophy and metaphysics that have helped him in his development both as a martial artist, and as a human being.

The Inner Forge: A Guide to the Martial Spirit
Apr 2013
ISBN 13: **978-1483958934**
What keeps us from the level of impact, devotion, and personal power that the masters of the past were so well known for? The modern world has lost something, a spirit of a sort, and this is seen as easily in the practice of the martial arts as anywhere else. Come join the author as he delves into not only what the martial spirit is, and what it is not, but also how one can regain this deep spiritual approach to the martial arts, and by way of that, all of life.

TABLE OF CONTENTS

Light of the Force
A Seeker's Guide

Introduction

- LIGHT OF THE FORCE -

Letter from the Author

I want to begin this book as I should have my first: I want to thank George Lucas for his creation. He has stated that he created the concept of the Force for people to examine the divine from a different angle, and he succeeded in that effort. The following of the teachings of the Force, and of the Path of the Jedi, have saved my life, and made me whole, as I discussed in my first book, *From Nerd to Knight.* At first, as with all who walk that Path, it started as a curiosity, a new framework for examining things around us. In time, either that framework does not fit us, or it reveals itself to be the best approach we can have for our lives. It is at that moment that it stops being a philosophical and metaphysical practice, and becomes what I call a religio-spiritual Way.

Without *Star Wars*, and the amazing impact that has had on the culture of the modern world, I don't know that I would be alive today. So, sincerely, thank you for the inspiration, George. Your powerful images gave me strength to survive an otherwise hopeless situation.

This book has been stirring in my mind for a very long time. I have walked the Path of the Jedi for more than a quarter century, and one thing that I realized is that so few people within that group truly understand what the Force is, and how it interacts with each of us. Because of that, much of the teachings of the Jedi seem very arbitrary, and sometimes even a bit hollow.

That sent me on a quest for information, and for understanding. I took to closely examining the religious and spiritual undertones of the Jedi of the fiction, in all media: movie, book, television, and game. Surely, with each source, the flavor changed a little bit, but I see that in the same light as any spiritual practice: relating specifically to a single person in different ways. I have taken the fiction and begun to see it more as a spiritual mythos, the fables from which we learn truths about ourselves, the same as with Aesop. We all know Aesop's fables, and we know that they were not meant to be literal occurrences, or real people.

They were stories told in a way to keep us entertained, and to open our mind. The media of the day is no longer limited to written word on page. Now, we have digital media, in all of it's various incarnations (video, ebook, web page, etc). Just because the presentation is so much larger, and obviously newer, that does not mean that we cannot find kernels of truth in these works as well. As the mythos continues to grow, so too does the possibility of understanding what the Force is, not in these fictional settings, but through the explanation of each author, as they can only describe what they can see, hear, and feel. That is one of these beautiful conundrums of the human mind: we don't really create, only adapt..

Not many people are going to agree with this statement, but the longer you walk the Path of the Force, the more this will resonate: I feel that these stories, and impact they have, are destined, and designed by the Force. Just as George Lucas got his inspiration, so too do all other creators... but where does that inspiration come from? Some say the mind, which exists in a state both inside and outside of our physical form. Others say that the inspiration for true creation comes from that which is beyond our understanding: the Infinite, the Unknown, the All.

The Force.

So, keep that bit of my personal conjecture in the back of your mind as you read through this book. The deeper you go in this, the more you will strip away the layers of society's taught doubts and fear, to see the truth. The Force is All, and it always has been. It has existed since time unknown, and will outlast all life in this universe. It wants to be knows to us, once again. This time, the inspiration came from a movie of wizards and knights, evil emperors, and the rebellious cries of the downtrodden.

Force Guide and Protect You.

JA Michaels

Into a Larger World

Greetings, fellow student of life. I can see that you, too, have been called to something more, something deeper. You may be a fan of *Star Wars*, and just kind of noticing a bit of disconnect from the world around you. You may have already broken away from the societal religious organization that you were raised in, because something felt off. You may even be a practicing Force worker, be it under that name or any other: witch, medium, druid, healer, seer, mystic, wizard, yogi, sorcerer, etc. There are as many paths to the Force as there are fish in the seas.

No matter where you are on that scale, you are here, reading this book, right now. Be mindful of that point. Something put you here and now. The odds of you doing anything different than reading these words in this instant are unfathomable. And yet, here we are, taking these first steps into this world of wonder and introspection. Take a moment, and bathe in the infinitely precise nature of such things. Feel the hand of fate, as it rests on your shoulder, as you peer down at these words. The world has conspired to put you exactly where you are, and there is something magical about that realization. As we dive deeper into the understanding, teachings, and practices of the Force, we will naturally grow a more internal, connected perspective on all aspects of our lives, and we will become so much more complete, and whole.

I started my journey into the Force in 1995, with my first steps into the Path of the Jedi. That, tied with my lifelong practice of the martial arts, opened me up to various spiritual teachings and energetic practices, of both Taoist and Shaolin variations. I have also trained in many different neopagan traditions, with heaviest focuses on

Druidry and Alchemy. These studies have synthesized into an understanding of my spiritual Path, which has always lead back to the calling of the Force. My foundation was always reinforced with this outside knowledge, but it was only when I was an active Force Follower, or **Forcist**, that I came to my points of greatest insight.

I need to say, right now, that the Way of the Force as I put to page, is my personal arrangement of years of study and experience. They have changed many times over the years, and they will likely continue to change, as is the nature of a living path. I do not claim to be a Prophet of the Force, or anything that extreme. Instead, I am merely a Child of the Force, spreading what I know with the world around me. However, this practice is one that I have refined through teaching, both live and digitally over the last decade, and have found that the method is sound, and helpful.

This practice is not the easiest to follow. It requires effort, and it will require intentional, directed change. It will require discipline, and perseverance. Most of all, it will require time. None of these practices will change you overnight. It has taken your entire lifetime to become who you are, so do not expect instant results from any new endeavor. The aim of the spiritual practice of the Force is a shift of the mind, towards understanding and the ever-flowing process of enlightenment. Even a mighty tree must first grow from a tiny seed.

Enlightenment is a bit of a loaded word to use, as it can mean many things to many people. There are some groups that see enlightenment as attaining clarity of all of the worlds wrongs, so that they might avoid them. Others, upon attaining enlightenment, are said to understand that the Universe flows in total harmony by its own design, and thus they are not needed to maintain that harmony. The Forcist sees enlightenment as a process, not a moment. I have often said:

Enlightenment is the balance of Ignorance, Intellect, and Insight.

This points to the endlessly cyclic, and flowing nature of enlightenment. It is a never-ending process that shows us that we are a part of the song, and the song is harmonious only because we are here to play our part. This shows a stark contrast between Forcist teachings, and the doctrine of other introspective groups, and that is to be expected. Spirituality evolves with the world, and as such, any spiritual path is going to echo the point in history from which it grew. Paths that developed during times of great and localized war often speak out against violence. Paths that developed during times of oppression will centralize to some extent on overall equality. Paths that grew in a time of ignorance, like the Dark Ages, centralize on both knowledge and understanding, two very different things. Paths that develop in a time of rigid conformity will often hinge on freedom of thought and personal expression. All things, when taken from the central point of harmonious balance, will strive to return to that point of flowing center. We will discuss this in further detail in the next section.

The mythos that spawned the Forcist teachings was developed in a time of unrest abroad. There was war, but at a distance, war looks more noble and sterile that it actually is. In fact, none of the movies have come out when the Western World wasn't at war on some front. The original movies came out in the late 70s, early 80s, during the overbearing shadow that was the Cold War between the USA and USSR. The prequel movies came out at the start of the War on Terror, and the most recent movies came out during the end of that same war action. That has caused the Forcists to look at the need for peace, and the study of non-violence, but at the same time, draws towards the study of self-preservation related acts of personal combat, not acts of large scale war. We are, by and large, safe in our detached understanding of the war actions around the world, and that affords us a different point of view than similar paths of old. It does not make us better or worse, but it also does not make us interchangeable with these other groups.

Another defining factor is that many esoteric

paths, most notably neopagan and pagan restoration practices, the integration and acceptance of modern technology is shunned from the practice. In that respect, a Forcist would be more aligned with what is called a techno-pagan: a practitioner of a non-Abrahamic religious and/or spiritual practice that does not shun technology. Again, this stems from the fact that most introspective spiritual practices grew out of a time before modern technology, and does not place them as lesser or greater. Just different. The actual practices do not speak against what did not exist at the time, but the traditionalists of these groups do push against the inclusion of newer technology to maintain purity in the action, which is noble in the effort.

The Force, as a spiritual practice, is aimed at improving all parts of the self. There are practices that require some level of effort on the part of the learner, and the long-time practitioner. Inability to do so doesn't exclude you from following this Path, but the unwillingness to do something that you *are* capable of will just lead to this being a sterile approach to the teachings, which will benefit you the least. That does not mean that this book is not meant for you, but there are likely better books on new age philosophy, and even *Star Wars* inspired philosophy.

As a matter of fact, this is the first book I have found to address the Force from within the paradigm of a Forcist, rather than simply making comparison between the tenets of the Force and other, older spiritual and psychological practices. The Way of the Force has been growing since the introduction of the concept in 1976, and it has not been without it's growing pains... but, now is the time to put words to page, to help those who seek to know better understand the Force as it presents itself to the world, here and now.

The Force

The Force: History & Mystery

The Force is far older than any name by which it has ever been called. Qi, prana, magick, mana, the divine, juju, the universe, the purple gumdrop in the sky... it doesn't matter. We all existed before we had a name, and we all exist as more than just the sound that society has decided to use to identify us. The same is true of the Force. Many people use that type of statement to merely equate the Force to other older, more recognized belief systems. I personally feel that leaving it at just that treats the nomenclature as merely a mask, like a form of cosplay Taoism. Instead, I like to look to these older concepts because they are all bits of truth. They each reveal a new facet of the whole. It is as if one looks at an intricate sculpture, but only from one side. Each different angle reveals something different about the sculpture, but only when we have seen as many angles as possible do we have a more complete understanding of what it truly is.

Unlike the sculpture, no one can know the whole of the Force, especially in one lifetime. To do so would be a grand attempt, but would undoubtedly end in failure. To know the whole of something would require that thing to be locked, stationary, still. The Force is none of those, for it is an infinite flow, an infinite transmutation of energy from one state to another. I have often butchered the opening stanza from the Tao Te Ching to better illustrate that point.

The Force that has been named is not the whole of the Force.

So, to better understand the great mystery of the Force, we look to those who have known parts of it. We look to understand the Force by seeing as many facets of the stone as we can, so to speak. When we study the core principles of these various belief structures, we find the overall connected truths, and those help us to better understand the whole of the Force.

Not everything is going to resonate, of course. That goes back to the point of each Path forming due to the circumstances of the time. The Force is in a constant state of flow, and exists as everything at once. As such, the Force that I interact with today is not the Force I will interact with tomorrow. The flow is constant, and thus change is constant. I have a fondness of seeing the Force as a river, and the way we interact with it is exactly the same. Water never really dies, nor is it truly ever remade. It changes from solid to liquid to gas, but it is all the same water. However, the element of water is so vast that there is almost no way that a person can ever drink of the same water twice. The Force is exactly the same, ever-flowing, ever-cycling, and on a scale far greater than anything our human mind can imagine. It is both finite, and infinite. It is finite in that the Force is all things, and all things are energy, which can neither be created nor destroyed. It is infinite in that it perfectly recycles all parts of itself, from potential to kinetic, and in all forms of growth and atrophy, showing that it is beyond the degrading affects of time.

Like any other discovery, the observation of the Force over the centuries has changed. With it, the name has changed a bit as well, but that is more due to language barriers than anything else. Human language has a very difficult time putting something as huge, perfect, and complexly simple into written or spoken word. As such, we tend to become very poetic in out explanations, and very limited in our ability to put a name to such great and awesome things. The mind just really doesn't have the words, sometimes.

So, keep the enormity of the All in mind as you read through this work, and see certain things borrowed from other sources, or only slightly modified. The Force is vast, and complete. The study of it should be vast and complete, as well... or at least as complete as possible from a subjective view.

The first time the concept of the Force was ever presented to the world was in a 1976 writings, and eventual screenplay. This low-budget filmmaker's passion project became something so ingrained in the culture of the western world, that is has spawned movements and subcultures world wide. Of course, that screenplay was first produced as *Blue Harvest*, the working title for *Star Wars*. In this day and age, you would be hard pressed to find someone who has never seen, played, or read some facet of this fantastic story. Let's look at this story, for a moment, and try to understand why it is so woven into the minds of the world.

We start with the story of a farm boy, born of greatness, but exiled to a life of hard labor and political disconnect from the greater universe.

He was isolated and unhappy, but he was safe, under the watchful eyes of his family, and his sworn hidden protector. In no way should this young man ever be put in danger, where he is. However, the Force does as it does, and brings galaxy-shifting events to his doorstep. He experiences great loss, and dangers he has no preparation for.

And yet, thought it all, he survives. He is lead by his hidden protector, now his spiritual mentor, through the trials and dangers immediately ahead, and then brings him into a cave, an isolated point, safely away from danger, and introduces him to the Force. He speaks *just enough* of the nature of the Force to give this sheltered young man the key to unlocking his potential

After the death of the spiritual mentor, the young man keeps growing, keeps following his instincts, and he finds over time that he can become a great Knight of the Force, and a Light Bringer. He had some help along the way, from another mentor, and a dusty old tome left for him, but he did the work to become more, to become greater.

He trusted the Force.

The Force had a job for him, and as such, it made the path ahead very distinct. That job was that this Knight of the Force would bring the Light of Balance back to the Galaxy.

Conversely, this story tells of the corrupted father, torn by his tragic past, and poisoned by the pain of loss. Though not seen, finding that his son was not dead began to stir his emotions in way that he had not felt since the day his son (and unknown daughter) was born. He thought they were gone, as was his dead wife. He mourned them in the most destructive way he knew how, but the story of the father is one of loss, and the corruption of his mourning by his manipulative master. The father was tragically out of balance, and was made to put his pain, and his self-destructive desires, out into the worlds around him. He had no control over his own past, and so he used that rage to bring total control over his future.

After the son grows into his true power, his true strength, faith, and connection with the Force, he saves his father from his turmoil. He helps this broken man heal his spirit enough to find peace, harmony, and balance for the first time in decades. We see the spark of the Light in the eyes of the dying man, not the hollow black mask of the cyborg.

Then, we see the youth and promise of the father, as if we are reliving his life at the moments of his death. We see his extraordinary life, and the pressure that was placed on him because of it (a mistake thankfully not repeated with the son). He wavered, and fell under the weight of an entire galaxy needing him to save them. He was born of the Force to secure the Light of Balance, and he failed in the immediate. However, his last actions as a living being, and his redeeming action as a father, did serve to destroy the center of the destructive imbalance in the Force, if only for a time.

We see that the Force brought him into being to bring balance, even if the method was not the happiest. The rise of the unified Imperial forces came from the broken, complacent government that it eventually destroyed. It was order, where as the Republic before it was corrupt, slow, and overall a ritual of pomp, rather than a body of action. From the ashes of the fallen Empire came a new, purer version of this Republic, in which all had a voice, and the actions of the body were fair, and swift, not bogged down by gears demanding grease, and politicians demanding payment.

It was messy, but the Force brought balance back to the galaxy. It took decadence, and replaced it with overbearing order, swinging from one extreme to the other, like a pendulum, until such time that the people of the galaxy found a working equilibrium. It wasn't perfect balance, but it was stable enough, if everyone worked at keeping it that way. That is how how active, dynamic balance should be.

I always prefer to look at the story from the macroscopic, removing the characters, and looking at the movements of each piece on the board, as if watching a master's round of chess. Seeing the story beneath the movie is very important as a Forcist. It is a skill we have to develop to better learn how to find the lessons that the Force is offering to us. Those lessons are not always from within the *Star Wars* mythos, either, because insight can come from anywhere, so long as it helps one to grow into a more complete personal understanding.

With that, let's begin to look at something very important to the understanding of, and growth in the Force. The Balance.

Ashla & Bogan and the In-yo

There are a few terms that we are going to have to go over in each of these sections. There will be a glossary of important terminology in Appendix A, as well.

We are going to start with the **In-yo**, the crescent shape at the beginning of each chapter. It is an older, lesser-known Japanese image to represent duality in all things, much as the more popular *yin yang* of Chinese and new age teachings. Both symbols share the same core principles. As a yin yang is half one color and half the other, the In-yo is also. The center circle (white in the example given previously) is meant to be exactly half the size of the outer circle (shown in black in the example). That means within the larger circle, there is as much black as there is white. There is as much *In* as there is *Yo*. The idea of *In* and *Yo* is one of complimentary opposites, no one being of more or less value than the other side. It is in this that we reach the harmonious balance.

The image is also thinner at the top, and wider at the bottom. This points to the waxing and waning of the Force within each of us. We grow stronger and weaker, both in the cycle of a single day, and in our lives as a whole.

This brings me to a misconception that has

been part of the Jedi Community since it's inception, and one that I am very actively attempting to correct, both here and actively with my teaching online. The Mythos never spoke of the "Light Side" of the Force. Only the *Dark* Side, and the *Good* Side. If we are to apply the In-yo concept to this, then that means that one aspect is Good, and the other aspect is Evil. However, in the In-yo view of the complimentary duality of all things, to assign the greater concept of the Dark Side to this format makes one side of that Evil.

However, as has been taught in Taoism, and many sects thereafter, no one side of the In-yo or yin-yang approach to Balance is inherently good or evil. To attempt to view such grand concept to the format of dynamic balance is short-sighted folly. It breeds a misunderstanding of the nature of the Force. In the earliest days of the Jedi Community, it led to some being berated and driven out because they could not fake some emotional disconnect, because to act with empowered emotion was "the Dark Side", which is just not the case. That leads us to our next point.

Ashla and **Bogan** are the terms for the Good Side and the Dark Side, for Good and Evil. The Ashla is found in the Dynamic Balance. That is the Light of the Ashla. It is at this point that things thrive, and flow, and vibrate at a higher level. The Bogan is active Imbalance. This is harder to explain without extreme examples, but the use of an extreme example helps us to draw sharp lines. When we know those sharp lines, we can better identify the thinner, blurrier ones. The Bogan is actively seeking to destroy the harmonious balance. It is bringing discord, and pain, and terror... all the things that root themselves in disturbance and chaos. To act of the Bogan is to intentionally lower the vibration of an area, and actively dim the Light of the Ashla.

Reading it, we all see images of atrocities. The corrupted father from the Mythos is a good example. He touched the Bogan, and fed into it more and more. He felt himself attaining his goals, and felt that would lead back to security and balance, when it only led to more chaos. However, that is not the only way that Imbalance can be pushed on people. For example, someone who is always super happy, and makes sure that they are never seen experiencing anything other than the most awesome time. That is called repression, and it will eventually cause some kind of fallout. Maybe it is depression, maybe destructive habits like substance abuse, maybe something far more violent. It comes from the forced imbalance. This is why we attribute the Bogan to something that the Mythos called the Dark, It takes effort to stay out of balance without falling. It is that fall that is the most devastating point for anyone walking the Way of the Force.

The Force has existed since time began, and likely before that. It will always return itself to balance. If we are fake with ourselves and others, we will eventually fail at that, as the Force will push us to return to balance within ourselves. The Force will bring itself back to the Ashla, as through the Ashla, all things thrive. That is the entire undercurrent of the

Mythos, all things return to their core nature, and all actions have the chance at redemption, even if we cannot see it all the time.

3 Parts of Self

Humans experience life in many different ways, but the vast majority of what makes people who and what they are can be found in the three primary forms of Self: the body, the mind, and the spirit.

The body is our physical manifestation, the meat suit that we get to maintain and pilot around as we experience this world.

The mind is our consciousness. It is the way we observe and learn. It is the medium by which we grow more aligned with the world around us.

The spirit is the little sliver of the Force itself, as we live out the subjective experience of the objective existence. It is through our spirit that we truly become all things. It is the connection we have with the rest of our greater self, the Force.

These three phases of ourselves are not always aligned. Think about any time that you learned a new skill. Your mind understood the action before your body could do it effectively. This is the lack of synchronicity between these two parts of ourselves, and that is pretty common. We lose synchronicity with our spiritual self far easier as we grow up in a world that actively tells us things like "it's not real" and "believe in only what you can measure". Both are very scientific statements, and have likely saved many people from serious injury or death over the centuries. However, that has come at the cost of the greater connection to the Force as a species.

We are not aligned together. We are not connected. As such, we are distressed in record number; unhealthy of body, tortured in our own minds, and our souls feel hollow as a cave. I am not aiming that at any one group. It is all of us, every living person in this day and age suffers from the doubt and fear that is brought on by having too sterile of a view on life. When we are alone, honest with ourselves in the darkness of night, we can each admit to some point of disconnect, some torment. I am no different.

Through practice, we can each find our way back to the Force. We can find our feet planted firmly in the river of the Force, allowing it to wash us clean our torments, so that we can become greater, become more. We can find those glimpses into the whole of existence as it truly is, that moment when we see all as the Force experiences itself.

7 Vibrations & Gateways

The Force manifests itself in all things, and human existence can only really experience part of the vastness of the All. We are, after all, just a small part of the Force. The unity of our body, mind, and spirit opens us each up to new experiences in the Force, and consequently, in the world around us. With each level of experience in the Force, we become more fully aligned with it.

Humans experience the Force in different ways, but there are seven major ways that we can observe the Force, and interact with it. The division between one of these vibrations and the next can be fuzzy at times, to the point that until very recently, I didn't even acknowledge them as actual vibration rates, but as transitional points. Many people will refer to these as various aspects of the Force, but I try to not create that level of artificial separation, as at the end of the day, it is but a small part of what we can experience of the Force, and even that is but a mere sliver of the whole of the All.

These seven vibration rates also correlate with the seven major energy gateways in the body, most commonly called chakras. The teachings of the chakras come from much older sources, and as I am not an expert on these specific teachings, I will not use that term so as to not confuse my personal findings with any other form of orthodox spiritual practices.   The connection between the Force as the All and the spiritual makeup of the Forceform, our energetic body, can be seen in Figure 1, shown here.

As we go further into this study, we must remember that these divisions are drawn to aid in our understanding of the All, not to limit it. Some will have a natural reflex to look at these correlations as steadfast divisions, but just as the various colors of light are different vibrations of photons, so too are these each just different vibration densities of the Force.   The Force is one, the Force is All.

Internal

The Internal vibration of the Force is the first that anyone ever really feels.   It is that inner wellspring of energy that helps us to awaken, and rise from the bed to face the day.   This is the most directly related to our physical health, as this is replenished through the metabolic process, and through sleep and meditation. It is an energy that is most closely associated with the concepts of safety and survival. Fear robs us of this energy vibration, which is why it can become such a crippling thing. When we lose this stability, we no longer have a strong sense of personal well being, which will diminish our connection to the Force.

This gateway, which we will call the Base Gateway, is found at the base of the spine. When seated in meditation, this is where the Force comes into our beings most strongly. It is the root of the tree that is our central energy system. This gateway is often associated with the color of red, the lowest vibration of visible light. It is also connected with the tone of the note G.

This is the very base of our entire sense of self, and is ten linked to the statement of "**I AM**." It's here that we build not just who we are, but who we would also like to become. When we begin

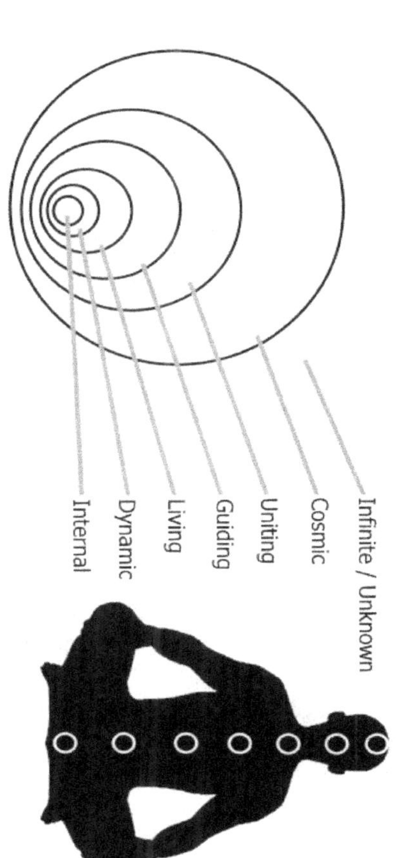

Figure 1: Vibrations, Gateways, and the Body

the journey into the Force, we must start here. We must take the time to enter into a state of self-evaluation, and set our course correctly, or we will not succeed. Many have begun the process of spiritual refinement on the Path of the Force, and countless more on adjacent Paths, because they were looking for some escape from who they were at their Base. They never took the time to correct their I **AM** statement to reflect the change they wanted to see in themselves. If we want to become more aligned with the Force, to be a true Forcist, we have to make the beginnings of that change every day, to reinforce our journey, so that we do not falter.

When this gateway is strong, we are empowered to grow and become greater. We move forward with a strong foundation, and the strength of a mountain. Because of this, we most often feel most connected to the element of Earth when moving from the Base Gateway.

Dynamic

The Dynamic vibration of the Force is the one most directly linked to the output of strength. As is inferred by the name, this is the active, and sometimes-explosive output of energy, such as in the practice of internal martial arts, or reaching beyond one's physical limits in a sporting competition. This is the core energy that drives us to do great and powerful things.

This vibration is associated with the Center Gateway, as it is found at the physical center of gravity for the human body, and also because it is the place where we must keep our emotions centered and structured, lest we be destroyed by their untamed fury. This is also where all creation springs forth. This gateway is associated with the color orange, as it is a denser vibration rate of light, and is connected to the tone of A.

As this gateway is linked to the way we process our emotions and creative energy, it is often linked to the statement of "**I FEEL**." This gateway is robbed because of guilt. We are, as a modern society, often taught that the things that we feel as children and teens are not important. Either it is our first tickles of the Force, and we are taught that there is no such thing and that we are imagining them, or it is some form of conflicting or confusing emotional state, where we are told that it is not important for our survival. Another way that can be robbed is by destroying creativity in another, saying that their skill is impractical, unprofitable, or not something that will be of use to them in their adult lives. This is why we must be sure to understand and nurture our **I FEEL** statements. We do that by looking inside, and just observing the flow of emotions, because emotion is the source of all creativity. We see them as they pass, and observe how they make us feel. When we find the moments where we feel like we should not indulge in an emotional expression, we must look at why. If we have learned that this type of expression is dangerous, such as a type of angry outburst that leads to self-harm, then there should be no guilt in keeping that response in check.

However, if we are taught to feel guilt over being happy, or over creating something of beauty, then we must look back to when we were told that such feelings had no merit, and we must release that guilt. We have to forgive those who told us that we were wrong, even if that person looks back at you in the mirror everyday.

Because of the constant flowing nature of this gateway, it is most closely associated with the element of Water. The constant shift and flow, ebb and swell, that can be found in the emotions at their rawest form closely resemble the nature of a flowing river. It also points to the danger of being carried away by this energy. A river is often central to an ecosystem, until such time as it floods and drowns all the life that it once supported, or dries up, and all life dies because it is no longer there to keep the area alive and thriving. The emotions are the same: vital to a healthy life, but destructive when out of control. As such, we must learn when to calm the river, and let balance be restored.

Living

The Living vibration of the Force is the essence of all living things, the heartbeat of the world. It is what builds all life, and what is amplified by all living things. This does not merely belong to the animate forms of life, though. It is in all plant life, all microscopic life, and even in most raw elements, All parts of the planet are alive, aside from overly-processed synthetic polymers, like plastics. As such, all aspects of the world around us exist, in some form, in the Living. It is the densest, and broadest vibration of the Force that we can access at this stage in the spiritual evolution of our species.

This vibration is associated with the Belly Gateway. It is here that we feel the sense in the pit of our stomach, that warning of potential danger. As such, this gateway is often associated with learned experiences that have developed into a type of social skills, and what is termed "street smarts". This vibration is also responsible for our willpower. While the Dynamic is responsible for our creativity, it is the Living that drives us to put our creation out into the world, It is what steels us for the road that lies ahead, be it good, bad, or yet-unknown. This is the vibration of the Force that our reality rests in, and as such, it is the easiest for us to reach and develop. It is also the highest of the gateways that manifest themselves in highly physical ways. This gateway is associated with the color yellow, once more stepping into an even denser state of visible light, and it is connected to the tone of B.

This gateway is connected with the way we exist in the world around us, and is linked to the statement of "**I DO**." This gateway is diminished by way of shame. Shame is not the same as guilt in that we may not feel guilt for the way we handle a situation with the best of intentions, but be ashamed of the outcome. This is where we become the victim of our own ego, and we beat ourselves up over mistakes that we have made. It does not matter how developed one is in the Force, or in their life: we all make mistakes. It is possible to do everything correct, and still fail. As such, we must be determined in our **I DO** statements, and allow ourselves the imperfection of being alive. Yes, you will fail at times. If you are not failing, then you are not doing.

Because of the powerful and transformative nature of this gateway, it is most commonly associated with the element of Fire. It is also centralized in the body at the center of the metabolic process, which is at its core, a burning of calories to keep an engine running. Fire is often shown as an element of pure destruction, but it is truly the Force's method of transformation. Through fire, crude ore can be formed into stronger metals for any variety of use. The fireball that is the sun gives the planet the warmth and light it needs to sustain life. Fire can be misused, but with any true transformation, there is a bit of risk, and a bit of loss. If there wasn't, there would be no need for the change.

Guiding

The Guiding is the understanding of the undercurrent of time, and how it passes. The Force is an active participant in the lives of those who find themselves in it. The more we align ourselves to the Force, the more actively it inserts itself into our Path. As such, we can learn to sense the flow around us, and oftentimes find the best course of action by simply being still and listening to the tug inside of each of us.

This vibration is connected to the Heart Gateway. This gateway is very important for people in the world currently. Our state of overall spiritual development makes this the most important step, because it is here that we begin to exist in a more complete way, as a child of the Force, striving for the Ashla, rather than just a person surviving in the world. This gateway is often said to deal with our emotions, but that is not completely accurate. This gateway deals with how we use the energy of our emotional states to better bring about the

Ashla, and to create balance within ourselves and the world around us. This is where compassion becomes such a pivotal point in our development as spiritual beings. Compassion is the statement of unconditional love and acceptance of things outside of yourself, so long as those things are not intentionally destructive. It is here where we begin to connect with other people, and the greater web of the Force. This gateway is strengthened by our ability to balance and harmonize our emotional energy. This is also the gateway that brings about the greatest amount of healing, as it is the one that usually holds the most intricate damage. It is often associated with the color green, the color of new life, and is connected to the tone of C.

This gateway is where we begin to grow outside of our ego, and to reach out to other people. As such, it is often tied to the statement of "**I CARE**." This is such a unique statement, because people often do not understand the depth of what it means to truly care. Compassion is the act of caring for other people with no expectation of reward. However, there are times where we invest too much of ourselves too quickly into a connection, and that leads to a possessive quality that is detrimental to true compassion. These types of connections oftentimes fail, and when they do they rob this gateway by way of emotional pain and grief. When we are plagued with grief, we shut this gateway off from the Guiding, and it can no longer lead us to where we are needed the most, or where we can do the most good. To combat this, we must be clear in our **I CARE** statement, not just in who we care for, or what we care about, but also how far we have the strength to dive into a problem. We are all still evolving, and if we care too much, or in the wrong way, our failings will bring grief, and we will feel lost. The Force will no longer be able to guide us, as we will not hear its whispers over our own pain.

This whispering, flowing, gentle nature associates both this gateway and vibration with the element of Air. It is difficult to catch air, and at times it will seem as if still, but air never truly stops moving. It is essential to us, as our breath, and it is essential to our development along the Path.

Uniting

The Uniting vibration of the Force is the web of interconnection that ties all forms of living energy together. We all exist in the Force, and of the Force. However, it is through the Uniting that we experience things *as* the Force. This is the way we learn to be of ourselves, and at the same time, be as an entire macrocosmic life form. Just as each of your cells is its own living piece, it is only through their interconnection that they become to living being reading these words. We are the same in how we experience things, and how we are universally tied to all other things.

This vibration is tied closely to the Throat Gateway. This gateway is a truly magnificent one, in that it gives us the direct connection to the web of the Force, and how it connects to all forms of life that we can understand and experience. It is through this that we learn the truth of reality is that all things have vibrations, all things have a heartbeat, in a manner of speaking. The web of the Force carries that sound from one point to all points, like the strings of a guitar. It is here that we learn how to pluck those strings, and when to not.

In many esoteric paths, this is the gateway, and corresponding vibration, used in creating changes in the Force. Chanting, prayer, or organized spell casting; they all call for the use of the voice to give the actions power. This shows the power of all words, and why we, as spiritual beings, should always be mindful of what we say, and when we should say nothing. This gateway is one of the expressed manifestation of the will, and the vessel of truth. Truth is always a very subjective thing, and as such, we may not always be completely factual in our wording, but as long as they are spoken with all the sincerity of our own personal truth, then the words have done no wrong. This gateway is connected with the color blue, and resonates with the tone of D.

This is the gateway that gives us connection with the wider web of the Force, and as such, it is what calls for us to present ourselves with truth and sincerity. It is commonly linked with the statement of "**I SPEAK**." To speak into the world is to speak into the Force, and to speak into the Force is to become an active voice in the vibration, the harmony, of the Force. This gateway is weakened by lies. Having facts incorrect is not the same thing as a lie. Lies are done with intention. Incorrect facts expressed without the intention to spread false information are simply errors. We must be clear in our **I SPEAK** statements. We must look within ourselves, and be sure that we are speaking from a place of personal truth and understanding. We must also be willing to humble ourselves enough to know when our silence is the strongest, and more correct action that we can take.

This gateway is tied very directly to the element of Sound, because living things take in sound at all times. Even those things and people which are unable to hear still take in sounds in the form of vibrations. We are always connected to the wavelength, the sound of the Force, and as such, we must be steadfast in our dedication to what we speak.

Cosmic

The Cosmic vibration is what exists outside of this plane. It is the astral, the fabric of space-time, and the Otherworldly home to all other forms of life. It is the Cosmic that gives us access to the realms of the spirit, and the places outside of time. It is here that we learn ourselves the most completely, because when we access the Cosmic, we can see all that is, and we are fully aligned with the Force.

This vibration is connected to the Forehead Gateway, most commonly referred to as the Third Eye. The third eye is a function of this gateway, but we do not want to limit our understanding of its entire function with incomplete wording. This is the gateway that allows us the ability to look beyond our understanding. All things exist in a state of duality: stability and motion, balance and imbalance, hot and cold, wet and dry, growth and atrophy. It is through this understanding that we better gain access to the Cosmic through the forehead gateway. Everything that we know has its opposite. That goes for the physical plane, which reveals to us the astral. Time is also subject to this, revealing to us that which is outside of time.

This gateway is also responsible for many of the more common "psychic" skills that people develop as they refine themselves spiritually. It is through the forehead gateway that we learn to truly "see" or experience the minute, and the divine. We gain a level of intuition that runs alongside clairvoyance, even precognition. It is a level of awareness that can turn a normal person into a walking sage, a mystic amongst mortals. This gateway is associated with the color purple, and resonates with the tone of E.

Because of this very powerful nature, this gateway is most commonly associated with the statement of "**I SEE**." Once again, this is not a function of the physical eyes, however as you function with the gateway awakened, your spiritual senses can easily work themselves into your physical senses. Instead, this is a statement of understanding of the larger puzzle. This gateway is robbed of its power through illusion, oftentimes the ones we build for ourselves. Hubris and ego are very difficult to get away from, and as such, the Forcist must be very clear in their **I SEE** statements, because it is just as easy to build a self-serving illusion as it is to break a limiting one.

The function of the third eye, specifically, is one that helps us to interpret the energy that we receive from other people, or beings not of this plane. It is through this function of the forehead gateway that we can interact with what many occult schools term "beyond the veil". This means breaking through the barriers of this plane to enter into that of the astral. The astral is the home of the Akashic records, the record of all knowledge from all life on this level of spiritual evolution, from both planes.

There is some debate as to whether the astral is the same as the Otherworld, the home of beings of legend, such as dragons, elves, the Fae, etc., but that is a debate for another time.

This gateway is very directly tied to our individual and collective link to the Astral. When first activating this level of connection, be aware that what you experience may be overwhelming. Manifestation is far easier in the astral, and such can become quite enticing. However, feeding this can become a type of illusion of power, which will quickly enough taint your connection to the astral, and take you out of alignment with the Cosmic.

Infinite/Unknown

The Infinite and Unknown is not a single vibration. It is the acceptance that we do not know all of the Force. We are limited in our consciousness, and even when fully connected to the All, we can not logically comprehend what is beyond our mind's ability to grasp. For example, no person can describe a new color. Even though we can access part of the Infinite and Unknown, and catch glimpses of these unknown and unnamed colors, we have no way to logically recreate them, or even describe them, because our mind is limited when we are in it. We must never forget that we are the subjective experience of the objective existence of the Force.

This vibration is attached to all of the gateways, but it peaks at the crown of the head. As the base gateway is the root, the crown gateway is the showering of limbs and leaves, bringing energy up, and out endlessly back into the unknown and unseen from which it was first drawn. It is through this gateway that we complete a healthy cycle of spiritual energy, and find our purest connection to the Force. In this gateway, we gain a level of wisdom beyond mere understanding. We gain moments of Oneness with the Force, and the moments of Enlightenment that come with that level of true harmony. Neither oneness nor enlightenment are permanent states, nor should they be. The

Force flows in an endless circle, and so too should we. This gateway is associated with the colors silver or white, and resonates with the tone of F

This is a truly unique and powerful connection, and this gateway is most often connected to the statement "**I UNDERSTAND**." Be careful with those words, because they are often misused. This is not an intellectual statement. This is a level of spiritual refinement that brings about a new perspective, and a new goal. Every time that we reach this point, we will lose grasp of it. That is because, once we are here, our spirit matures, and with that, so too does our goal of oneness. This gateway is robbed of its power by unhealthy and/or codependent attachment, be it to a person, object, or even a life situation. At some point in our lives, we will all get to a point where we have grown comfortable without being complacent, and we will count on our circumstances to have some level of stability. The second that we expect that, we have grown that attachment that strips us of our connection to the Infinite.

This gateway is unique in that opens a direct connection to the flow of the Force, and as such, there is no other way to vocalize how that is experienced. It is a complete state of awe, and understanding, and mind-racing, and emptiness. It is completely connected and aligned to the Force, as much as any person can. Each time we reach this point in full effect, it changes for us, and we are changed by it. It is the epitome of transformation, and the experience is never lost, but almost impossible to hold onto for any length of time.

That is not to say that we lose alignment with the crown gateway, because we don't lose it just because it is not overwhelming. It is like seeing for the first time of the day. Everything is bright, and you squint against the glare, but eventually, you no longer have to squint. That is what happens. We open this gateway, and are overwhelmed by what comes through, so we squint against the glare, we push against the overwhelming rush, until we are comfortable with it, and then begin to open ourselves a little more, growing more comfortable each time.

These vibration phases of the Force are important to know, because they do play part in how we evolve spiritually. However, at the end of it all, we must not let these distinctions become divisions. The Force is All, and no matter what level of spiritual refinement each of us are at, we are still children of the Force, and all it's complex simplicity.

The Cycles of the Universe

The Force is the same in all things, both big and small. What exists in the minor also exists in the major. This can be seen by observing the cycles of our lives, and the world around us/ We each come into this life frail, grow in strength, and fade away. That is the nature of life, and can be seen in the In-yo found at the beginning of each chapter: we start at the top, where the line is thinnest, grow powerful in life, and eventually fall into atrophy, once again becoming frail, before we leave this plane. This is a cycle echoed in the smallest of organisms, all the way to the expansion and eventual collapse of the known universe.

As we grow more complete in our connection to the Force, we should look to acknowledge and observe these cycles of growth and atrophy. Many occult traditions do this by following a solar calendar, paying reverence and reflection for the Solstices and Equinoxes, as they mark the transition from growth to decay. Our ecosystem teaches us that, even if it seems that all things are dead and gone, the Force remains, and thus life returns.

This should not simply be observed in relation to the seasons, or the cycle of human life, but look even smaller. The lunar cycles represent the same flow and ebb, as they affect the tides of the planet every night, and bring about a cycle of renewed light each month, breaking the darkness. This observation of cycles leads me into this next point.

The Force and the Life Cycle

There are many outlooks on what happens when we leave this level of existence, and return to the Force. My study of the mythos often offers a confusing view, with the presence of apparitions that act as guides, but also the statement that these guides cannot hold this state, which they now call The Gift, indefinitely. This speaks of some form of an afterlife where those found worthy can maintain their character, and even ascend the restrictions of the physical, to become far more powerful beings. However, that is not the case with most, so where does that leave us?

As the various vibration phases of the Force correspond to the older teachings of the chakra system to a rather eye-opening extent, we must also look to that framework for a better understanding of what happens when we die.

My meditations have revealed to me that we exist in the strongest connection to one of the 7 phases of the Force. When life first began, it fought to stay alive, and built itself up, generation after generation, until a single cell became a vibrant and complex life form. In that state, life is inconceivably small, and aligned with merely its survival. That makes the beginnings of life on this plane connected to the Internal phase of the Force, that which is our core, and how we process the Force from one form to another to stay alive.

After that, we began to develop into mobile forms of life, able to interact with other life forms, and our environment. Life began to become active, and thus connected to the Dynamic phase of the Force, learning how to use our processed energy to move out into the surroundings.

Next, life became aware to some extent, and learned that there is both connection and division in all different forms of life. We began to develop into different types of life: animal, vegetable, fungus, and mineral. The further we go, the more complex we have become. This is when we first aligned with the Living phase of the Force.

Next, we entered into the stage of complex consciousness, the age of reason. That is where life as we know it is currently. We are learning about everything that we can observe, directly or indirectly. We are learning how we are all truly connected in ways that we cannot directly observe, but we can observe the effects of through experimentation. We are most aligned, as a life cycle, to the Guiding. We are *very* attuned to the Living, but we are learning to become more completely aware of the Guiding, which is what this level of the life cycle is for.

Beyond this stage, we will enter into the vibration of the Uniting phase, where we will learn to blend ourselves into the fabric of the Force, and become both the subjective and the objective at the same time. That is where The Gift resides within the mythos, and why one who has it will become more powerful than one can possibly imagine, to borrow a phrase.

Beyond that phase, we enter into harmony with the Cosmic phase, and we become what people would consider gods, but only because of the dramatic difference in the way our perception and understanding would work. This phase is where we learn how to be all, know all, and create all. This is where the beings known as the Celestials existed in the older portions of the mythos.

Lastly, we enter into a level of development that cannot be put into intelligible words, as is revealed by its name: Infinite and Unknown. What is there is the All, the Force. This is where we return to the objective, having all the complete knowledge of the subjective, and thus shedding any need for the difference.

— — —

So, that is a bit to wrap the head around, but it is actually a pretty common system of understanding the spiritual evolutionary process. It is necessary to understand a few other points along this process. The Force is Infinite not because it is endless, but rather because it is perfect in its recycling of energy. Energy can neither be created nor destroyed, only changed.

The same is true of all sentient life, and it can be seen by looking below us. Our physical shell, when left to break down naturally, becomes nourishment for the soil upon where we are laid to rest. All those things that we once took in for energy are now taking what energy is left in the shell, recycling them for the next generation.

Our mental and spiritual energy are the same. If we have developed enough to ascend into the next state, into the Uniting phase of the life cycle, then our energy is moved from one level of enlightenment to the next. If we are not yet done, we are put back into the system. Our spirit exists in this moment, in this life, and is not totally suited for any other life. As such, parts of our mental energies and spiritual energy are broken up, and used to build what I call new spirit characters. A person may inherit 99% of a previous lifetime, but never 100% without intense spiritual understanding of the process, and amazing enlightened control, such as His Holiness the Dalai Lama, and without seeing the process from the outside, there is no guarantee that even he is getting 100% reincarnation.

However, a higher percentage of a single spirit can show itself in memories from past lives. Those are not always memories in a visual form, or in a way that can be written. Sometimes, you will have an uncanny understanding for some skill you had mastered in your previous incarnation.

To bring this back to a point, the Force wastes nothing. If we are ready to ascend, some or all of our spiritual existence will move on. What doesn't move on will be left in this phase, and be used to build new spirit characters, so that all parts of all beings can learn all they must know for this life.

As for the Gift, we exist in a vibration now that we can see and observe the levels of less complex life, and with a little effort, we can communicate with this, for their benefit and ours. We can speak increased life into a plant, and we can learn the wisdom of years by sharing our energy with an old tree. We can learn the practice and benefits of fluidity from the flowing river, and we can learn how to be strong beyond compare from the mountain. Because we can commune with the less animate forms of existence beneath our vibration phase, so too can that phase communicate with our phase. This is where we find our spirit guides, our ancestors, and the otherworldly.

Practices

Forcist Practices

Knowledge of the Force is a pivotal first step in the life of a Forcist, but it is only the beginning. Knowing the map is not the same as walking the road, and as such, to truly become aligned with the Force in our lives, we must take the steps along that road, boldly and without fear. As with many spiritual paths, this includes many practices that, alone, may seem a bit dogmatic. However, the practices of the Forcist presented here have been found to be powerful tools in the development of a strong, and beneficial connection to the Force, and the world around us all.

Many of these practices have their root both in the mythos, and in the inspiration for the mythos, in the spiritual practices of old. None of these practices are terribly new in their use, but the combined use of these various tools are unique to the teachings of the Force. When these practices are taken from the mythos, they are employed because they hold benefit to the goals of the Forcist in how they develop themselves, and how the practices benefit their interactions with the world. These are the tools of healing of the student, so that the student might better serve the Ashla, and bring harmonious balance to the Force around them. Every journey begins with a first step, and everyone will stumble along the way. That is why these practices are often simple, yet powerful tools to self-development.

What is listed in this section is not all of the practices that a Forcist can adopt in their daily lives, but these make up the basis for a solid foundation from which we must all grow into our own unique expressions and connections to the Force.

Guardian's Mantra

There are many mantras, codes, and creeds within the mythos, and all of them hold some benefit to the development of a student. This has gone to create several more within the online Jedi communities, but some of those are built upon a dualistic, flawed understanding of the Force, and as such are of little benefit for the spiritual development of those who employ them. Most are tailored for their respective sects of application of Force teachings, such as the Jedi, Sith, and even to some extent a Mando'a creed. There is only one of these creeds that fit the direction and goal of the Forcist, and that is the mantra of the Guardians of the Whills. I have slightly modified the wording, as it was presented in a broken form in its introduction.

I am one with the Force, and the Force is with me. I hold no fear, for all is as the Force wills it.

I am one with the Force, and the Force is with me. That is a powerful statement, and one that everyone should ponder at great length. This statement shows the connection of the Forcist with the whole of the Force. It is here that we learn that, even within the mythos, it was seen that all forms of life were seen by some as the subjective expression of the objective All.

I hold no fear, for all is as the Force wills it. When studying this creed, I modified this from the original statement of "I have no fear" to "I hold no fear". This is because, simply put, we are all imperfect beings, and we do have fear. Fear is a spiritual enslavement, and the mirror reflection of hope. If we fear something, we are hoping that it will not be as we expect, even if we cannot put that negative expectation into words. Rather, we must acknowledge that fear, and release it, because all is as the Force wills it.

This mantra, as it was used more often than not within the mythos, points to something that few people really ever want to discuss, because it seems wrong to say out loud. If we hold no fear, and fear is the hope against a negative expectation, then we should also let go of hope. Hope is often used to mask an insecurity, or a dream that something outside of ourselves is going to hand us something good and empowering. However, we must remember that we are but a very small part of the overall of the Force, and because of that, the Force does not really care what we hope for. That means whatever we pour into merely hoping is dreaming, and a bit pointless.

The Force is active, and flowing. So, rather than hope for something to come, or change, we must jump into the flow, and bring about the change. The Force is an active participant in the lives of those who bring themselves closer to it, but it rarely changes things just off of a hope and a dream. Instead, do not hold that hope, either. Make it a heading, make it an active goal. Then, the Force moves with it, and all things are as the Force wills it. Become a part of that creation, that process of manifestation. Be one with the Force, and the

Force will be with you.

This mantra is a powerful guide into understanding and growing into a strong and stable relationship with the Force. If you hold onto nothing else, and you put all that you are into these few words, you will be better aligned to the nature of the Force than most.

Dedication

When starting a new part of our personal journey, many spiritual practices have specific rituals for beginning that path. There is often the sacrifice of something personal to the student, and some form of oath to be true to the teachings, as they are presented by a teacher, or group. The study of the Force does not demand such things of anyone. However, it is not a bad idea to write up a personal contract with yourself, committing yourself to the methods and practices of the teachings of the Force. Many have found over the years that this type of personal dedication to a task has helped them to stay on course, and keep an open mind to the teachings as they receive them.

In a world of digital, instant information, it has become easier to get distracted, and bored with a topic that takes time. This causes people to quit walking any Path that doesn't offer immediate results. It is not anyone's fault. We have become conditioned to having everything right away, and immediately available to us. Working on the depths of the self is not a task that can be taken lightly, should anyone wish to get anywhere. Here is a sample dedication that anyone may use, or not use, or modify to their personal liking and purposes.

On this day, I dedicate myself to the teachings of the Force, and the Forcist Path.

I take this step, knowingly and willingly, to better myself, and the world around me.

I dedicate myself to the Ashla, and the betterment of anyone in my Path.

I will study the mysteries of the Force, for knowledge and personal refinement.

I will strive to be an ever-present force for goodness and right in the world, every day.

I will walk my Path at all times, and keep myself humble while staying honorable.

Modify that as needed to fit your circumstances, but don't make it too easy on yourself. Hold yourself accountable for becoming more, because no one else truly can. From there, write or print it, sign the page, and keep to that which you have pledged yourself to. Should you decide to take this route, the level of ceremony attached to this is up to you. However, keep in mind that ritual and ceremony, while not needed, do aid in a greater impact in any spiritual or other esoteric action, rather than just printing it out, and taping it to your door.

So, should you decide to take such action, go

big with it. Spend some time in meditation, and plan out what symbols you may want present. Many esoteric groups call for representations of their pantheons, but there is no pantheon of the Force. As such, we often do not do elaborate ritual totems. Most times, a simple candle to represent the Force, or a pair of candles of contrasting colors, to represent the harmonious balance of the In-yo, showing the active balance that is the Ashla. Bells and singing bowls are also very common, as well as incense and things of that nature. These are all symbols from the paths that helped to inform the foundation of the Forcist teachings, and thus they are viable parts of a person's individual practice.

The more elaborate the setup, the more time it takes to build the experience. That means, the more energy you pour into the experience, which builds expectation, and impact. It is pouring the Force into the ceremony meant to dedicate yourself to the study and understanding of the Force, as best we can. This actually brings me to this very next point.

Robes and Garb

The spiritual tradition of ritual garb dates back as far as anyone can remember. The garb could be as simple as a wrap made of the skin of a sacred animal, or could be as elaborate as colorful studded robes of silk and leather. The purpose of this garb has always been somewhat the same. The human mind changes slightly when we wear certain clothing. Think of the businessman, who always wears a suit and tie, and is always laser focused on making deals, and producing a profit. Now, see that same man get home, and change out of his work clothes, putting on a pair of comfortable pants and a loose shirt, so that they can relax. They are not concerned with making things happen, but are far more content reading a book in a comfortable chair, or watching a program on the television, allowing his mind to relax. We have to ask ourselves, why did he change out of his suit? It was already wrinkled and worn in from the day, so why not just stay in those same clothes when at rest?

The answer is that he could not relax fully still in the clothing he wears while working. This same phenomenon can be observed in the training halls of the traditional martial arts. The students all wear a uniform that has little practical modern equivalent, but because of the conscious act of changing into this uniform, they have altered the way their brain is processing their day. They are, ideally, no longer worrying about what is happening outside of the training hall, and can give themselves fully to the lesson, so as to release the stresses of the day, and refine their bodies in ways that the modern world rarely calls for.

The comfortable clothes of the businessman, and the training uniform of the martial arts students, these are the garb that represents the task they are dedicating themselves to. These are their ritual garb.

Spiritual practices often call for a suspension of daily woes and stresses, so that focus can be more absolute on the practice at hand. This is why the Forcist is highly recommended to adopt the idea of robes. Now, the term "robes" in the mythos conjures an odd blend of monk-like cloaks and tactically-minded clothing, with sturdy boots, and a leather utility belt with pouches for various supplies needed in the field. This is not what is meant in this context. Instead, the term robes here is more free flowing, and comfortable. It allows for unhindered movement, and comfort over a long period of seated meditation, or standing practices. Think less space wizard, and more Shaolin or Wudang monk. These are the ritual garb of a student of the Force. They should reflect the simplicity of the Forcist, as well as the harmonious balance of the Ashla.

My personal robes can be seen on the back cover of this text. They are built of a black pair of loose fabric pants, and comfortable white tunic, and a gray outer tabard, or long vest, tied closed with a simple white sash. In the picture, I am not wearing shoes, but when I do, they are simply comfortable slides. Aside from the tabard, these are all parts of various martial arts uniforms that I have from my years of training, but they don't have to be the exact same. Loose pants and shirt, one part darker and the other lighter, would do just as well. The important aspect of this is that the items are comfortable enough to wear for extended periods of time, yet remain special in that they are not worn for daily lounging, or seen as some type of costume.

The reason for this is that energy builds up on things over time, and they take on a feel of their own. The more often that you dedicate something to the same form of task, the sheer donning of that item will begin to align you to that task. Just as a work uniform would get us more in the mindset of our daily occupation, so too does the wearing of ritual garb help to center us in the actions as we take them.

Once a Forcist decides upon a set of training robes, they become the garb of all personal rituals. Should an item wear out, as things tend to do, the replacement of that item will alter the feel of the ritual garb. For this reason, they should not be worn in any context outside of training and personal ritual. As mine are mostly martial arts uniform pieces, I will wear them during my physical training as well, aside from the tabard. However, I have their matching pieces, white pants and black tunic, for my more strenuous training sessions, so as to safeguard them.

Lifestyle Refinement

Going back to the made point that many spiritual paths require some form of ritual sacrifice, the ways of the Force do not. However, it is *encouraged* that the student make steps towards improving their lives. The obvious first thought is one of dietary change or restriction, but there are no specifics involved in anyone's diet that are called for. Eating cleaner, healthier food is always of benefit, building a better overall health, and reinforcing the physical vessel. The stronger the body, the stronger the connection to the Force in that body. That doesn't mean that someone with a physical weakness of incapability cannot have a strong connection to the Force, just that we should always strive to improve ourselves everyday, and cleaner eating habits is always a good place to start.

As important as eating habits are, those are not the only encouragements or recommendations for a better alignment to the Force. Removing other toxins, such as smoking, drinking, or use of illicit drugs are also powerful ways to build a better, stronger self. Undertaking regular forms of exercise is also of vital importance.

The goal isn't to become an Olympic level gymnast, or some cross country runner. If that is where you end up, that is all the better, but the goal is merely to push for improvement. Become better than you were. Push yourself just a little bit further than you think you can, so long as it does not lead to injury.

Once you get into the teachings, you will see that the goal is to get better. A one percent improvement everyday is an amazing transformation after a year. It doesn't have to be a massive push, it just needs to be improved..

Remember, the Force is with you, because the Force is you, and you are the Force. Follow where it leads you, and if it leads you to rest, then do so, just so long as you feel that it is the Force, not merely the ego screaming about having to change, or being uncomfortable, or any other multitude of things.

Physical Combat Art

This brings me to a very important point on this Path: the Forcist is expected to make themselves physically more capable people. That is often accomplished through the use of martial training, be it weapon-based or empty-handed. This does not include twirling choreography, because there is no understanding or expectation of danger involved in that type of recreational practice.

That understanding of danger, to self and others if misused, is vital to the spiritual refinement of a Force follower. We cannot truly appreciate an item until we know how heavy it is, physically or metaphorically. The modern world has made itself too safe, and because of that, few understand the weight and responsibility of the dangers of the world. They are never prepared for it, and because of that, when situations arrive, they become a far greater shock to the spirit of the one caught unawares.

Back to the point, the training of some martial discipline is pivotal to the development along this Path, and many paths like it. It teaches body, mind, and spirit unity, learning to flow as one entity, not three disjointed aspects of one clumsy lump of flesh. The Forcist path draws from a martially-focused mythos, and that undercurrent is present in every presentation of the Force within that mythos. Even the dedicated spell-casters within the mythos were combat trained, as they were of a powerful race of warrior witches.

Drawing from history, there are many groups of warrior monks that, while spiritually aligned with the divinity of all life, trained in the arts of combat, such as the Buddhist monks of Shaolin, and the Taoist priests of Wudang. Both took the training of combat as their avenue to true and total peace and control. It seems a bit illogical to find peace in the training of combat, but only on the surface and only when seen as merely a physical action. When one can attain emptiness, and effortless flow in a state as chaotic as one-on-one combat, they have truly mastered themselves, and are unshakable. The purpose of the Forcist is to find this point of center, and active stillness, even within the illusion of chaos around them at any given time. Should they find themselves in a situation where they must act, they must keep their center, or the Force will fail them in their time of need.

Now, this is not to say that anyone with physical inability cannot walk this path, but that is the importance in knowing the difference between an expectation with exceptions, and letting the exception become the expectation. One pushes people to do better, to reach as far as they can, and maybe even a little bit further. The other doesn't push the mind of the Force follower, and fails to act as the catalyst for personal change that is needed in order to find one's most purified self. For those who face physical struggles, many schools of physical combat arts are well-versed in adapting their teachings to those who may not have typical capabilities. Do not be afraid to venture out, and look.

The overall goal is to bring the flow of all parts of the self together into a cohesive whole, prepared as one can be for anything that may happen. We have to first learn to find harmonious balance in all parts of ourselves before we can learn to exist as an extension of that within the Ashla.

Forcist Staff

In the modern world, it can be difficult to find good training in some parts of the world. Some areas do not allow for the training of dangerous weapons, such as swords, or the large machetes of the Filipino martial arts. Those weapons, while formidable, and truly fantastic training tools to learn the weight of the reality of danger, can also being prohibitively expensive in some areas. As such, the weapon most recommended for the Forcist is the staff.

The staff is the perfect representation of the path of the Force follower, as well as the most common path associated with the Forcist, that of the Jedi. It is a weapon of nearly-pure defense, holding no offensive characteristics, such as a sharpened edge, and can be used in a wide variety of ways, depending on simply shifting grip and angle of stance.

The staff is easy to come by, versatile enough

to find a replacement for in a pinch in public, such as a broom or mop, and is most commonly made from wood, thus linking it to the living cycle of nature, and acting as a natural connection enhancer to the Force.

That also points to an important part of the Forcist Staff: it is not always used as a weapon. There are often times where it is used as a focusing tool, to better hone and direct Force projections, as we will get into further later in the book.

There are many ways to come into possession of a personal staff. One is by directly purchasing one. Wooden martial arts staffs, of various lengths and wood varieties, range anywhere from $25 to well over $200, depending on many options. A 1" dowel, purchased as a local hardware store, may not be a combat grade hardwood, but still makes for a fantastic focusing aid and physical training tool. Just remember to sand it smooth, because splinters are a good way to ruin an afternoon's training. There is always the chance of receiving one as a gift, as well, but the most direct and powerful way to come by a staff is to go and cut your own.

There are also a wide variety of media dedicated to the training of the staff. Books and video are readily available from various sources, and dedicated to art forms from various regions around the world. The staff has been the world's most universal weapon for the length of human history. Many have devised ways to use them. Spending time in reflection on how the staff is employed can help to decide what training path you will take. It may be that the most direct training option is not the most spiritually-aligned method, as it may focus on overly-increased levels of violence, or flashy competition twirling with no meaning to the movements.

Do not let that dissuade you. You are the one who decides how you use the skills you gain. If you need live instruction, take the hyper-violent training, and bring it into balance within yourself. If the only option is twirling, supplement the physical training with books or video of more defensively-minded training systems, and find the combative principles within the dance. With the right mindset, anything can be grown, changed, and evolved to be of benefit. The purpose isn't to merely learn one side, or the other. To have true balance in the practice, we must reinforce both the martial and the art.

There are specific rituals involved in bonding with, and awakening a Forcist staff, listed later in this book.

Breathwork

The body is the vessel of the Force, and as such, it should be kept as strong as possible. Directly connected to the practice of physical combat arts, there are breathwork exercises. These exercises can be found throughout history. They exist as things like tai chi, qigong, and yoga, just to name a few. They are both passive and active art forms, and train the body, mind, and spirit as one. This helps to being the student into a greater connection with themselves, and through doing so, gain a level of attunement and clarity within the Force and how it interacts with them. This is a gateway to understanding our specific place in the Force. However, the physical health benefits are also of great importance. The gentle nature of many of these practices in their beginner stages offer a slow building of the body to handle the next stage of difficulty. Before long, we are doing things with our bodies that we had no idea we could do. These skills also help us to learn to better control the flow of the Force in our body, as well as how to direct it to specific tasks, such as clearing a blockage, or healing an injury.

It is beyond the efficiency of written media to teach these such skills, so this is going to end the discussion on the specifics of this topic. Just know that the Force follower is recommended to seek out this information, either through live instruction, or through other forms of interactive and visual media. There is a plethora of information on these types of practices available on the internet.

Affirmations and Self-Hypnosis

Another practice of the Forcist is one that has a much longer history that most know of in the greater occult and esoteric communities. That is the use of affirmations. Affirmations, if you are not familiar with the practice, is reminding yourself to not allow limiting thoughts and behaviors to steal your personal power, your center, or your connection to the Force by way of seeding deep, crippling doubt.

As we enter into a path that is so focused on the refinement of inner self, and the connection to the Force, we stir up our own little limiting thoughts and behaviors. Most people call these their "demons", and that is a pretty good description for them. The person has lost control over these limiting behaviors because they allowed them to grow into something far greater than what they started as. After time, the behavior has crippled the person to the point that they cannot just muscle through the behavior, and are instead possessed by it. Yeah, demon really is a good word for it.

Affirmations are a form of self-hypnosis, and act as a gradual exorcism of those personal demons. It builds a light inside of the spirit that can be used to burn away the limiting behavior. However, these affirmations have to be built a certain way to be of benefit, and the process takes time.

The practice of affirmations is looked down on by some older spiritual and esoteric traditions because they most readily see them painfully misused, or sloppily created. The wording is simplified from something powerful and eloquent to a more basic, layperson writing of the concept. However, there is something in the flow of the more complex statement that makes it more impactful. In fact, it is the complexity that gives the statement its power. Let us look at an example. First, the more complex statement:

You are a being of pure radiance, spreading your light to all corners of existence to comfort all those lost in the dark.

Now, the simpler version:

You are a shining star for all to see.

Those are the same statement, at their core. However, the first one has more imagery in it, and because of that, calls for more attention when reading it, as well as more focus when saying it aloud. The brain has a slightly more difficult time with the more complex sentence. Thus, we focus on it more, pouring more energy into the words as we read and/or speak them. That, by design, makes the statement more powerful, and by that measure, is a form of rewriting the way the mind works.

So, when approaching the concept of affirmations, you can do some research into the more commonly used phrases, but remember that the more you have to focus on the statement, the more impact it is going to have.

That does not mean that you have to always use long-winded affirmations, either. If a very short one says everything that you feel it needs to, but it does not have the impact you feel it should, spend some time in meditation on the phrase. Make it a mantra for this meditation, and explore the depth of simple language. Pour yourself into the words, and that will put that level of impact into those words in the mind as you use the affirmation.

Another practice is self-hypnosis. That sounds way more complex than it really is. The practice of self-hypnosis is one of repeated visualization, where the Forcist builds an image in their mind of them performing a task they may not be very skilled at. Build this visual in the mind with as much detail as possible, and repeat it over and over again, gradually improving in the mind as you go. Let's use a staff technique for an example. Feel your limbs move, and your muscles contract. Feel the ground under your feet, and feel the staff in your hand as you repeat the technique time and time again. Studies have shown that this type of mental training is almost as effective as performing the actual action, showing that the mind is the ruling factor in any new skill. The more often you work a skill in your mind, the more your mind gets used to the coordination of the action. The only thing this does not build is muscular dexterity, because the muscles are not being actively used to perform the action, but when refining a detailed skill, or sequence, once the movement is learned, the body can build around that far better than building during tragically flawed practice. It is better to train the mind to refine out bad technique before we train it into our bodies, as well.

Now, do not take these statements as a reason to not actively train in whatever skill you are using for the practice. Instead, keep in mind, going back to our example, that you are not just learning to move a staff, you are learning how the staff also moves you. There needs to be some bio feedback during the process. This is just a way to better refine the fine motor skills in the mind between sessions of training it into the body.

33 Stones of the Force

The History of the 33 Stones

Many years ago, while writing my first book, I had many experiences where the Force spoke through me to put words to page that I had to later decipher, and explain in a way that not only made sense to me, but also made sense to pass onto the next generation of Force followers.

At the time, the words were written for the Jedi Path, because there was no clear division between that and the pure Path of the Force. Over the last decade, that divide has grown clearer, and as such, I came to the realization that these words were not meant for the Jedi, but rather for the spiritual practices of all followers of the Force, no matter what life path they set on top of the teachings of the Force. The Jedi Community, by and large, either felt these teachings too esoteric, or just discarded them altogether as too personal for the Path of a Knight.

As time has shown me, that belief was likely right. As the teachings of the Force were relegated to a secondary focus for a time, the 33 Stones of the Force have proven, time and again, to be immensely important in my own life, and growth. The original teachings that I had attached to these 33 points of development were tailored to the audience it was originally presented to, which truthfully restricted their meaning somewhat. In this presentation, there are no taboo dogmatic beliefs to limit these stepping stones, as they show a road map to the development of a Forcist.

The 33 Stones are unique in many ways from other teachings of the Force. While the number 33 is often found in modern neopagan texts, and the master number root of 11 being equally as common, these points were not made to fit those numbers. I merely wrote down these bullet points, and filled them in as I went. The number, and all that it represents, were of the Force.

In numerology, the master number of 11 represents a spiritual awakening, or spiritual evolution. The high master number of 33 is tied to spiritual change, and the changes that your elevated vibration will bring about in the world around you. Think about these points as you work through the following stones. These are not defined techniques, because the Force comes to each of us in our own unique way. They are rather things to watch out for, so that we may know where we are along the Path to the top of the mountain.

As we begin to walk the Path of the Force, we will find the first of these 13 stepping stones in a relatively common order. There are, of course, some minor variances, but these first 13 stones are pretty common in this presentation. You may have already taken a few of these steps, as well, as a few of the intellectual concepts have already been covered in this text. No one exists in a vacuum, and if you are still reading this book, there is a strong likelihood that this is not your first look into the teachings of the Force, even if under one of its countless other names. However, simply understanding these stones is not enough. They must be internalized, or they are just words on paper. For now, though, let's begin, and see where we each stand along that Path.

"I am the Force"

This is a statement of powerful understanding. Many religious practices draw a defined line between the practitioner and the divine source. Because of that, they have built in a clergy that is meant to act as the go-between for the layperson to interact with, and get guidance from the divinity of their religion. The teachings of the Force, and many similar esoteric Paths, are not like that. We come to an understanding that not only are we followers of the Force, children of the Force, but we are also made of the Force. We are the subjective experience of the objective consciousness of the Force. We are the Force, the All, in a limited physical form, so that it can better learn itself from all possible angles and experiences. That makes each of us the Force, and being of the All, that makes us all of one existence. All things are the One thing. I am the Force.

Unhooking the Ego

Many people begin a spiritual path in search of something that they are missing, or seeking to rind themselves of something that they do not like about their personality. These are noble aims, but in order to begin this process, we have to learn how to remove the ego from our self-reflections. Our ego does not like to admit to its own weaknesses, unless those admissions give it something that it wants. When we begin the act of personal spiritual refinement, the Force does not see your ego, as that is just an echo in your mind. The ego serves a purpose in keeping the logical mind accepting of an outside voice having some input into what a person does, or how that person exists, but it stands in the way of connection to the higher mind of the Force. As such, to truly become open to the Force, we must first look at our self image, and break it apart, removing the bluster of the claims of the ego. Only then can we see our true self, and present that truth to the Force.

There is no Dark "Side"

Within the larger Force community, this concept is one that gets covered quickly, but poorly. It starts with the statement that the Force simply is. It exists in all states, and does so at all time. It is everything, and the idea of light and dark are constructs of the subjective mind. That is, on the surface, true. However, as we learned in the first stone, we are the subjective experience of the Force, and as such, we are supposed to judge things for their value of light and dark, or good and evil. Then, the idea is presented that all actions, no matter the label, are present within us at all time, and there is no dark side of the Force, merely a dark side of each person. Again, this is true on the surface, but it still locks all aspects of the Force into a sense of duality, While knowing duality is what opens us to the parts of the Force that we cannot truly conceptualize otherwise, this idea limits the view, and that is partly due to the terminology of the mythos. Remember, the term the light side was never used in the original mythos, only the good side, and the only way to know the good side from the bad was when one was calm, at peace, passive. That means that the good is found in the balance, the Ashla, and the dark was found in the chaotic imbalance, the Bogan. Ashla and Bogan are not sides of the Force, they are states of the Force. They are harmonious balance, and destructive imbalance.

Force of 3s

The subjective experience that is human existence is made of three parts: body, mind, and the spirit, our point of personal connection to the Force. This is echoed in many different religious and spiritual studies, the most common being the Holy Trinity as adopted by Catholicism, and the Three Treasures of Taoist qigong practices. They both make connections between the body, mind, and spirit. The Force moves in us the same way, as a physical expression, mental projection, and spiritual experience.

Meditation as a Way of Life

One of the most common practices found in the teachings of the Force, under any name that it has ever been known, is that of meditation. This is the practice of training the body, mind, and spirit to all come to a point of unified stillness. Once that stillness is found, only then can the three parts of the self move in a unified state intentionally. However, meditation holds many other benefits for those who take up the practice. It helps to regulate moods, and steady the nerves. It can be used to help mitigate pain, and increase focus. Some meditation practices can even be used in place of sleep for a short time, as needed. Learning to quiet the mind also allows us to swim in the rivers of the Force more freely. It can bring about fantastic insight, and can even be used to confront trauma from the past. These examples are but a very small portion of the benefits of taking up meditation as a daily practice. If I were to list them all, this would be a much larger book. In the Appendix of this book, there is a listing for a fantastic meditation guide that you are free to look to for more modern insight on the practice.

Physical Discipline

Taking up a physical discipline is one of the most important aspects of being a Forcist. Because of the connection to the mythos, that type of discipline is most often the practice of a martial art, or some other form of internal practice that also trains the body. This is ideal, but the truth of the matter is that the body must be strong to maintain a powerful connection to the Force. The stronger the body, the more aligned it is with the vibrancy of the Force as a whole. We are the subjective vessels of the Force, and it is our charge to keep the body working as best that we can. Taking up any form of physical discipline that pairs itself with Forcework is the goal, but the training of the martial arts may not be a capability for some, either due to physical limitations, financial means, or mere social availability. In that event, there are plenty of other internal exercise methods that one can undertake. It merely requires a little trial and error to find the one that fits the best.

Expand the Mind

We are here for the Force to experience itself, and so that we can grow as the subjective, and the objective alike. To this end, we are charged with training our minds to become sharper, faster, and more educated. Through the expansion of the mind, we learn more about the world, and thus more about the myriad of ways that the Force expresses itself in this plane. As we walk our path through life, the Force will put information in front of us, and it is our job to take in that information when and where we can. Only then can we make use of that information, because many times, the Force will put us in a situation where that knowledge would be used, and to fail at that test is to fail our calling to the Force. That does not call for punishment, however, as we are limited and imperfect. We must take those times as lessons, and push ourselves to be better, and do better in the future.

Trial of the Spirit

This next point is going to sound a bit harsh, but the Force will break you, so as to better learn your strength. There will come a time that something in your life will go very bad, and your mettle will be tested. The Force is not punishing you for any failure, because at the core of it all, the Force does not really care. It does not play favorites, nor does it pick on those that it does not like. We may be tested because of some energetic or emotional baggage from earlier in life, or maybe a previous incarnation. This is meant to give you the ability to break the chains of that painful past, or that tormenting mistake. Whatever the reason, your spirit will be tested, oftentimes more than once, before you truly achieve this stone, because it is not the trial that is important. The trial is merely the method of testing if a person has learned a lesson. We all have lessons to learn in this life, and the Force becomes more active in the spiritual refinement of those who become more actively aligned with it. So, take the lumps, and find your strength to rise above. If you fail this test, worry not. It will come to you again, when you are ready to face the fire once again.

Connection to the All

It has been discussed several times that we are merely extensions of the Force, and as such, each thing in existence is also of the Force. However, that is just the first layer of the stone. Knowing that we have a connection to all things is an important first step towards development of a connection to the All. In this moment, you lose all boundaries of who and what you are. The artificial boundaries of your existence falls away, and we are no longer a person in the Force, but we truly find that moment of Oneness, and we become the Force. As we are still bound to this physical plane, we cannot maintain this connection at its fullest intensity, but once you feel that you are the universe, the astral, the past, the future, the known, and the Infinite... you become changed by that experience. You also become far more aware of how your actions, or inaction, can affect the world around you.

Breaking through the Veil

This is the experience of seeing with more than just the eyes. It comes from the initialization of meditative trance states to look into the astral, and see what others cannot see. It is often done with eyes closed, so don't expect to be walking down the road and just shift into this altered state of sight, where you begin to see the beings of the Otherworld. That might become possible after time, but in the beginning, know that you will likely not experience it in this way. However, the experience is important, so that we might learn to trust our instincts when we feel something nearby, or a pressure in the back of the mind. There are beings on the other side of the astral veil that have things to share with you, to better aid you on your journey, such as spirit guides, or even our ancestors. There are also beings within the astral who act as spiritual gatekeepers, made specifically to test those who approach the understanding of some hidden truth.

Inner Alchemy

Alchemy is the process of breaking things down into their most basic components to purify them, and rebuild them in a more complete and pure form. This is something that every spiritual path has to some extent, although the practices are not always branded as such. Life-changing experiences brought on by guided meditation, perspective-shifting ritual, even extreme practices, such as long-term fasting, or abstaining from sleep; these are all forms of employing the methods of inner alchemy. However, the process doesn't have to be grand. It can be accomplished by reading something that triggers a realization in your mind, or it can be simply slipping into a point of perfect stillness at will. These are all processes that take time and repetition to become good at, and so this stone, once you have stepped on it, you are not likely to ever stop practicing what is teaches you.

However, let's look at a more simplified example. Let's say that you have a weakness to high caffeine drinks. Caffeine is an extremely addictive substance, and kicking that habit can be not only difficult, if can be physically taxing. Some people will just try to quit cold turkey, but that seldom works for long. To approach this from an alchemical practice, take the time to look at what you get out of the substance: you feel less tired and sore, you can get more things done throughout the day, and perhaps it is something that you adopted because of a serious amount of work that you have to do during any given day. After you have found the root of the dependence, begin to remove a little bit of it each day. For example, a melatonin supplement to help get deeper and more restful sleep, to combat the fatigue from caffeine withdrawal. Beyond that, the use of some herbs for a more natural pick me up, such as ginseng, could help alleviate the need for high doses of caffeine. Do this process slowly, to minimize the pain that such a chemical withdrawal can cause, as well.

The alchemical process is not instant, and it will take several repetitions to properly cause a permanent change in your behavior, so give it time.

Resonance

Resonance is when we learn to not only hear the sound of the undercurrent of the life around us, but when we learn to match it. This is how we can quickly blend with an area to purify it, and become more at one with it. This will aid in finding life in an immediate area, because most forms of life do not fall into perfect resonance with their surroundings. You will not be able to do so, either, but with practice, you will get better. The closer you get to the living sound of an area, the more part of that area you become. Becoming one with an area is an important step in the forging of a personal sanctum, or learning to harmonize with the spirits of nature, as well.

To hone this skill, first start by entering social situations that you are not accustomed to. If you are introverted, but expose yourself to outdoor music festivals with lost of people, for example. Do not allow your contradicting nature to shut your aura down. Instead, expand it into the area, and mimic what you feel, like singing along to a song on the radio. Become more aligned with the energy in the area.

Some of you will not have trouble with vibrant, extroverted settings, but that just means that you have to find something against your nature. If you are okay in crowds, but don't like a bunch of unexpected outbursts, go to a sporst bar during a highly-anticipated sporting event. If you thrive in active settings, push yourself to become at peace in a bookstore, or library. If you are a city-dweller, find an outdoor place to become at one with. As we progress, we will all need to go into these various places, and allow ourselves to become less ourselves, so that we we can become more connected with who we are in relation to the rest of the world.

"I am the Center"

One of the most important practices that we learn is how to find our center. That is the point in the Force where we are more purely attuned to the Force in ourselves. This is reached when we take that a step forward, and learn how to act from our point of center. In that state, we move effortlessly in the Force. We see all that needs to be seen, hear all that needs to be heard, and move from a state of pure fluid balance. It is in this state that we are most actively attuned to the Force. This is when the Force informs our actions, and is guided by our needs. It is a difficult state to maintain, as it requires all abandon to trusting the Force, and knowing that it will put you exactly where you need to be, when you need to be there... and you are just along for the ride.

━ ━ ━

These next set of stones are far less structured in how they present themselves to each of us. We have to be more open to these, as their lessons can be much more specific, and could be of a greater importance to our immediate situation or development. The unique part of this group is that these lessons could have come before someone ever starts down a dedicated spiritual path. They may have even served as the impetus to that journey, so as you read through them, keep in mind that you may have already reached these hallmarks. There is also a possibility that, while these stones have been reached before that you must go through them more than once to learn the entire depth of the lessons involved. The Path is endless, and while we may not always be taking steps up the mountain, we are always taking steps forward.

Point of View

We all have our own developed perspective on life. This comes from many factors, including social standing, upbringing, and changes from powerful events in our lives. One of the most important things to remember is that, as the subjective experience of the objective All, each of us will see things differently, as we each stand in a different place in the Force. We may even view the same statement or situation to be drastically different things. We must keep in mind that these differences make up each person's individual truth, and we should strive to learn to see things from the eyes and footing of other people. We strive to understand the Force as it strives to better learn itself. The way of the Force is to strive to see all facets of the crystal so as to better understand the whole, the All.

Kindness as a Crutch

As we develop on our Path, we will grow in sympathy and empathy to the pain and struggles of our fellow lifeforms, human or otherwise. This will drive us to become more giving of our time, our energy, and ourselves. This is important on the path of the Forcist, because the Force is all things, and to be unkind to any part of it is to be unkind to ourselves, and the Force. However, there will come a time when our goodness and giving will be taken advantage of by others, oftentimes unintentionally. Some people are at a point in their development that they cannot find their own inner strength, they will naturally be drawn to those who have that strength and are willing to offer it.

Offering a helping hand to those who truly need it is the pinnacle of altruism. Helping someone when they do not have the strength is a powerful gift. That gift must also be paired with the knowledge and understanding of how that person is growing and healing, so that they may be strong enough to act without aid. It is the same as a child learning to walk. Help pick them up when they first fall, but if a parent never allows the child to push themselves back to their feet, they never develop the leg strength, core strength, or coordination to do so on their own. At this point, that continued act of kindness becomes a detriment to the development of the child.

We are all children of the Force, and as such, we must know when to stand back, and allow a person to struggle, so that they may become strong enough to rise on their own.

Eyes of the Force

We are limited by our physical form, and by that nature, we only experience things directly from the limited perspective of our existence. Through meditation and introspective study, we can learn to open ourselves to a greater experience of the world around us, and become more open to the nature of the Force in all things. The subjective point of view still plays a part in the experience, but what we develop is a level of connection that we can sense things shifting in the currents beneath the visible world.   We   can   observe   Otherworldly influences, as they interact with the energies of this plane. We can even begin to experience the scars in the Force in an area of great pain, or trauma. Some people can even visually detect such things, with little or no aid. We learn to look with more than just our eyes, because the limitations of the visible spectrum often creates illusions that can blind us from the truth in any given situation.

Hearing the Whispers

All things in the Force have a sound, a tone, but there are times that the Force will reach for your attention directly. You will hear a voice call to you, but it is as much as scratching of the wind in your ear as any tone, indistinct yet undeniable. It often takes the form of a genderless, possibly even singsong voice. It will call to you in times of great peace, great importance, and great turmoil.

Once this occurs the first time, you will also become more open to the words of those of the astral: Otherworldly beings, spirit guides, guardians, and things of the like. You will learn to hear the pain and joy of the lands, the wisdom of the wind, the knowledge of the flowing waters, and the expression of flame. These will not always present themselves as the mental processing of a sound, but you will still hear the words of the world around you, and you will know their message in your very core.

Opening the Inner Eye

This is a process of self-reflection, where we look into ourselves for trauma, imbalance, or any other limitation that may be keeping us from growing more fully into the Force. This also is the process in which we can access the memories of our spiritual past, and previous incarnations. Through this, we can learn important aspects of who and what we are, and how those parts of our being, often underutilized, can benefit our continued growth in the Force. The Force teaches us that we are all things, in all times, in all places. This is how we learn to read the history of our spiritual makeup, and thus the history of all. We can even go back to the first instant, the moment before all things, and see the creation of everything from everything before.

Disconnect

This is a terrifying step that we must all take, at some point. The Force will close itself from us, usually by way of some drastic shift in our daily lives. We will lose our connection to everything, and we will sit alone, in the darkness of nothingness. There are some that feel that this point is needed as we go through some powerful realignment within the Force, so that the changes do not bring us to the point of madness; and this could be true. Any time we experience a disconnected moment, we are often left in a point of bewilderment, until such time as our connection opens back up, and we experience the Force in all new ways. Often, we will feel as if we are starting over, learning to open ourselves to the Force once again, but that feeling is quickly replaced by a new level of integration and understanding. Whether the disconnect is caused by the collapse of personal illusions, or it comes as a needed reboot of our spiritual system, know that this step is often needed for us to grow, and become more aligned with the will and nature of the Force. Do not fall into despair, because the Force has not abandoned you.

To Move Beyond

One of the most interesting steps on the Path of the Force is this stone, where the Forcist is pushed to move beyond the teachings of the Force, and venture off into other spiritual practices as a replacement, rather than as a supplement. It is often connected to feelings of betrayal, loss, or simple boredom. However, stepping off of the Path is absolutely pivotal to gain the understanding of whether you are on the right road for your spiritual needs. The Force flows in all directions, and in all things. The teachings of the Forcist are not the only teachings that can be followed to reach the top of the mountain, and to attempt to push that upon yourself or another person is an action of repression, and directly against the core teachings of the Force.

Return to the Root

This stone is often seen as the conclusion to the previous stone, but that is only one of the ways this step presents itself. Yes, when one returns to the teachings of the Force, that fits this, but there are other layers. There are times when someone who practices the skills offered to us by the Force can get so caught up in the complexity of some actions that they forget to sharpen their beginner steps. A good example is a person who focuses on understanding the flow of time, and how that is woven into the fabric of the Force. They stay in a state of conjecture and introspection, unraveling this mystery, until they have lost their ability to bring a state of center, to find that moment of calm stillness. This person may then set down their mystery, and start back at the beginning, which is an entirely new journey, because the mind that started the Path the first time is not the same mind that is starting it anew.

Spirit in the Force

As we grow in our connection to the Force, and the world around us, we will begin to change, and to see things from new perspectives, and through new lenses. We learn a new understanding of the meaning of living energy, and how the science of the modern world limits our minds to a greater understanding. Once we do this, we begin to change, to evolve beyond the crude matter of our physical existence. We begin to fill ourselves with the pure energy of the Force, and that becomes part of our new state of being. We raise our vibration to a point that we can no longer go back to being what we once were. This is when we leave part of our being, or essence, in the rivers of the Force, and that part of us is always connected to the All in a greater degree than when we started on the Path. Our way of thinking shifts, our way of speech shifts, and our way of relating to others shifts. We become more enlightened to the underlying nature of all things.

Mentor, not "Master"

When a person discovers a truth that helps them to grow, they are often driven to share that truth. It is one of the most important parts of living as a Forcist, the sharing of understanding. However, this can be a treacherous part of our road, because once we see the depth and breadth of our personal truth, we know in our being that it is *the* truth. Once we know enough of *the* truth, we begin to feel as if we have all the answers for everyone. Again, sharing our understanding is of vital importance to our path, because to teach others is to learn how others see, think, and feel.

The danger here is feeling that your truth becomes the absolute truth, of which no one person can ever truly possess. Once we begin to mentor others, there will be some that fawn over our understanding, and come to the Forcist for clarity in all their problems. So long as they are not asking for the Forcist to solve those problems for them, there is little danger here, so long as the Forcist remembers that they, too, are merely a student of the Force. They must never forget the importance of not knowing, because it is that not knowing that allows us to further grow. Once you find someone who is in need of your guidance, never become a guru, or master. Merely be a fellow traveler, and walk the Path next to those you mentor, never in front of them.

Forge Your Blade

The path of the Force is closely tied to the path of the warrior, as both come from a point of self-improvement, the purification of the spirit, and a quest for understanding. As such, we must maintain the mindset of a spiritual warrior, even if one does not undertake the practices of martial training. We are warriors against ignorance and delusion, in ourselves as well as those around us who may be harmed by those illusions. We make it our job to break through these layers of incomplete knowledge, and social misinformation. We must be ready, able, and most of all willing to stand against these points, so that we can help to bring about a better world, without and within. To do so, we must harden ourselves to the task of breaking through barriers, and striving to become more complete in our understanding of the world in which we find ourselves.

The Sharpening Stone

As spiritual warriors, we must keep ourselves sharp, and capable, In the world of the physical warrior, that is done by honing combative skills. In the world of the spiritual warrior, that is more akin to honing the gifts and skills offered to us by our increased connection to the Force. These are mostly the commonly-termed "psychic" skills that are afforded us by our increased understanding of the interconnection of all things through the Force. Through this, we are geared to push back against destructive imbalances, be they directed or incidental. That nagging feeling that you can't shake; the sense of dread in the pit of the stomach; sometimes, even very distinct senses of dread. These are all points when we, as spiritual warriors, have insight into the hidden flows of the world, and we should be practiced at using those skills. We can help to heal the spiritual and emotional wounds of those we encounter, and we can best intuit when our aid is needed, and when it is a detriment. We must constantly strive to empower these senses, as well as our connection to the Force that reinforces them.

Becoming the Emotions

The Force is all, and thus, all things are of the Force, including our emotions. However, emotions left unchecked can be hazardous to our spiritual lives, and potentially even dangerous to the physical form, as well as the physical well being of other people. The emotions create turbulence in the Force, disturbances in the balance, and because of this, they must be fully integrated into ourselves, so that they act as the protective action that they are meant to be, rather than left to be the disturbances that rob us of our center, and make us ineffective when we are needed. We must spend the time to dive into the emotions, and experience them to their fullest, so that we can know how to act when in these emotionally charged states. This will also offer us the ability to more quickly calm and sooth these emotions, until they no longer present themselves as outbursts. This is not a point of repression, but merely a level of unified control. Release the emotions is not the same thing as bottling them up, which is done in times of need, to be expressed and released in a safe time and environment. This should not be first attempted until ready, as some emotions are powerful disturbances, and can do more harm that good to dive into before truly prepared.

Finding the Key

This is when we find the bridge between intellect, intuition, and insight. This is when we begin to break into enlightened states. Thinking becomes nearly instant, and finding solutions to questions that we did not know. This is often also associated with finding ways to subconsciously access the Akashic records, gaining knowledge instantly, as needed. Such is typically only for simple information, as specialized knowledge often requires some foundation to build upon that is not directly connected. This is the unlocking of the various parts of the mind, linking the consciousness to the subconscious, and those to the higher intellect of the Force. The first time this happens is often lackluster, but as the connection grows, so too do the results. Oftentimes, one may not recognize their having achieved this stone until long after it has manifested itself. Sometimes, this stone is not seen until it manifests itself several times, because of the subtle nature of such things.

Walking Between Worlds

This speaks of the ability to not only see beyond the astral veil, but also to interact in that other place. It is here that we learn to manifest in both realms at once, and how to better commune with beings from the Otherworld. It is this step that allows us to bring balance to those being influenced by astral disturbances, be they intended or otherwise. While we may not take our physical body into the other plane, we gain a fully realized representation in this spiritual world, our Forceform made as solid there as our physical form is on this plane. This is also a key point to the skill of dream walking.

Compassionate World

It has been discussed that the Force does not hold favorites, and that is true. It does not care about us in a compassionate sense, any more than a person cares for the struggle of a single cell in their body. It is not a statement of negligence, merely of scale. However, the Force flows in a state of harmonious balance, the Ashla, and in order to maintain that balance, we must strive to limit the amount of disturbances in the Force around us. This is done by elevating the harmonious balance in the world around us, by being compassionate to all life. That does not merely mean active life, or animate life, but *all* forms of life, down to the smallest insect, to the planet itself. We must show the world that the best way to relieve itself of its pain, is for each of us to help elevate those around us, so that we might all become more complete, and vibrant in the Force. In this, we bring our self closer to the balance of the Ashla, and we bring the life around us more wholly into the Force.

Seeing the Forest Beyond the Trees

This stone speaks to being able to read intentions, rather than just actions. There are people in the world who act in ways that are not how they present themselves. They may look like fantastic people on the surface, and say all the right words, and all the right knowledge, but still have the underlying desire to misuse what they have, such as seeking power as a means of control over others, rather than control over the self. We learn to see the incongruence between the person on the outside, and the person on the inside. Be mindful, however, that everyone comes from somewhere, and not everyone comes from somewhere wholesome. These people may be working to improve that conflict within themselves, and so we should not be quick to judge. However, knowing that the conflict exists is a valuable point of information. We may be in their Path to help them resolve that conflict, or they may be in ours for the same reason. Take things as they are, but with reaching this stone, we are now more able to see what truly is.

Tell your Tale

This is an important step along the 33 stones. It may be one of the *most* important of them. The teachings of the Force are timeless, and many have been echoed throughout human history, but the mythos that has spawned this particular incarnation of these teachings is quite new to the world. It is still mired with connections to the fandom of the fiction, because the world has not seen enough of the

Path to see the division held between the concepts of "the mythos" and "the fiction". This tends to push some people to not speak openly about their studies and revelations in the spiritual practices of the Force. This is not a point of anyone telling you that you have to go out into the world and tell everyone that you are a Forcist, just as no other spirituality expects their followers to run around and tell the world of their own unique, personal choices.

However, we must know how to tell our tale. We must know how to speak the words, and show the truth in them, and how they have helped us along our lives. At some point, you will be driven to share this part of your life with another person, or a group of people. You may receive a little ridicule from those whose minds are closed, but you will also receive sincere questions from others. Those answers may be exactly what others need to hear on their personal journey, and without your story, then they may not find the right answer at the right time to help them, now. The Force spoke to us, and we act as children of the Force, where we must speak the lessons we have learned, so as to help the world become more.

These last two stones are a bit bigger, and more difficult to put into words. It can take years to reach them, and some may never actually break the threshold of what they represent. They are also typically temporary states, and often lead to transitions in the life of the Forcist who reaches them. That is not to say that they are not worth reaching for, but more that their purposes are very specialized, and one may never be called to act in the way that these stones are used. However, we must also know what they are, so that we may be ready should the Force ever call on us to act in these ways. As a child of the Force, we are meant to become something greater than ourselves. We must be prepared.

Crystallize

This is a stone where everything that we know, and everything that we have experienced, blends into one instant. In that, we are not merely in the river. We are the river. We are the water, the shore, the forest surrounding the flow, even the riverbed. We are every stone in the way, and every disturbed current, as the river corrects itself. This is a point of ascension, of total connection, and it is momentary, for it would be maddening to be otherwise. This takes all parts of ourselves, purified and flawed alike, and locks them into a single point, a single sensation, a single experience. We see ourselves as the Force sees us. It is a point of judgment and evaluation. This is when we become who we are meant to be at any given moment, and learn the perfection in our unique flaws, and the successes in our failures. This is the state of Oneness. Some Force followers, and those of adjacent paths, have even said to begin to emit a glow, or a sound, when reaching this point.

Avatar

We are of the Force, and the Force is an ever-cycling river of energy. As such, things shift from one state to another constantly. The change may be minor, therefore the transformation may seem slow, but it is always there. This stone is a rare and difficult state where we are made to stop the nature of that flow in an area for a time. We have to become so aligned with every aspect of the Force in a given set of circumstances, be it a physical location, a group of individuals, or a length of time, and we have to stop it's free change. Instead, we have to create change. All forms of manifestation work like this to some extent, but those are usually using the river to aim the changes. This is placing a dam in the river, to divert it's flow to somewhere or something that is needed to stop a moment of escalating imbalance. Our action in this state is a form of imbalance in itself, but it is used not as a point of destruction, making it an act of Bogan.

Instead, the action is a point of counterbalance, restoring things more forcefully to a point of harmonious balance, thus making it an act of the Ashla.

This is a point where the Forcist gains levels of control that are typically outside of what is afforded to any single being, and we are driven to become the commander of the flow of the river, rather than a participant. We are the objective and subjective, the micro and macro. We act as a representation of the All. However, we must realize that we are not privy to knowing the entirety of the Force, and as such, our actions must be taken so that we restore the harmony, and then let go of this type of control. This state is often fleeting, but it can feel like riding on a shooting star. It is a power that can cause great harm to a person over a great length of time, and can feed any lingering desire for power and control. This stone, this state of total connection, where we are a living personification of the will of the Force, is exhausting: physically, mentally, and spiritually.

This is not a gift as much as it is a burden that we are willing to shoulder, should we need to. It is never a goal to reach this state, as it can cause great harm if we make even a single misstep. We risk our lives, and our state of centered well being, should we be called to this state of action. All of our training, and all of our experiences along the path of the Force are barely enough to prepare us for this state.

This state *can* be reached through intense meditation, but should never be sought after, because of the potential harm it can cause to the student, should they gain access to this state before fully prepared. This is a state that comes in times of great need. It is, in essence, the perfect spiritual weapon, and much like any weapon, we must be careful when training to wield it, and respect its power, should it ever have to be deployed.

Meditation

Purpose of Meditation

Meditation is a vital part of any spiritual practice, because it is in this action that we learn to quiet our minds, and become more fully aligned with all the parts of ourselves. Meditation has a wide variety of practice uses, as well. One such practical benefit is stress reduction, which can lead to a reduction in blood pressure, a serious problem in our overstimulated and caffeine-driven society. The intentional quieting of the flowing nature of the mind can bring a great deal of peace to the practitioner, allowing them to learn to better let go of daily stresses, and release that tension from their bodies. Another benefit is the practice of mindfulness, being totally aware of what is going on around you, and what that means both to you and for you.

Through prolonged meditation, the student can even learn to bridge the gap between the conscious mind and the subconscious mind. This is extremely beneficial if the student is plagued by nightmares, because most often, dreams are how the subconscious mind expresses itself. The closer the connection between the logical waking mind and the subconscious mind, the less often it will intrude in your sleep. I myself have actually stopped dreaming most of the time. When I meditate less, I find myself getting broken sleep, and having confusing dream states. This, of course, is not to say that we should aim to lose our dreams, but it has been known to happen, so be aware.

Meditation can also aid in some of the practices listed in the previous chapter, such as self-hypnosis. It is also the direct pathway to trance states, which are pivotal for advanced journey and Inner Temple work, something we will get to shortly.

The act of intentional stillness can also have profound changes in how we interact with the world. For example, there was once a study done at a civilian shooting range, where half of the instructors were asked to meditate, and the other half were not. Both groups were seasoned instructors, and were used to being in an area where firearms were discharged regularly. The half that were asked to practice meditation showed a dramatic decline in flinch reaction to the sound of the weapons being fired than the ones who did not. As they learned to find and hold their calm center, they gained a level of reserved detachment from the surroundings and situations they found themselves in.

However, daily practical benefits aside, meditation is the direct access to the mysteries of the Force, and how we bring those skills to us, so that we might learn to make them part of ourselves. We can relate meditation to a pool. We begin swimming in the shallows, where we can touch the bottom, and are safe while we learn how to operate in this new element. Once we are comfortable in the shallows, we learn to swim out into the deep end of the pool, knowing that we are still relatively safe, because we can always get back to the shallows with a little effort. Next, we dare to swim out into the river, where we can still see the shore, but we are now subject to the current of the Force. All of this leads to swimming in the oceans of the Force, into the depths where we must trust in our skills, and our connection to the Force completely. It is in this area that we risk getting pulled under, lost to the depth and wonder of the Infinite Unknown, and we must know how to pull ourselves out of that. This is all done through progressively more intense meditation.

If this is your first time meditating, it is recommended that you begin a meditation journal. List what meditation techniques you tried, how successful you were, how long you tried, and what brought you out of it, such as a set timer, or some large distraction. This will help you to see your progress, and there are some people who need that documentation to judge their growth.

However, we must not get ahead of ourselves. We must begin where all things do, at the first step.

Meditation Techniques

We are going to start with the most simplified meditation practice that I have ever found to work consistently. It is the first step in learning to let go of what is around you. After this, while I will be offering instruction for various forms of meditation, they all begin at the same point, and so I will not go into as great of detail. Don't worry, though. This step is pretty easy, even if you have never meditated before in your life.

You are going to close your eyes, and focus all of your conscious presence on one single point: the tip of your nose, between the nostrils. You are just going to pay attention to the sensation of air as it tickles past your nose.

In. Out. In. Out. In. Out.

That's all there is to it. Do not worry about counting your breaths, or holding it for any length of time. Those points come a bit later. All you need to do now is simply breathe.

In. Out. In. Out. In. Out.

Your body will rebel. It will scream in phantom pains, itches, distractions, concerns, even ridicule that we were all subjected to over the years. Let them come close to your mind, but never let them settle. Just blow them away.

In. Out. In. Out. In. Out.

Sooner or later, you will lose everything, except the observation of the breathing. No worries, no discomfort, no stress, no doubts. All of you will fall away, and all that will be left is the tip of your nose.

In. Out. In. Out. In. Out.

This is a pretty simple, and efficient practice, but it may not work the first time. However, given a bit of practice, and a bit of patience, it will definitely work.

If you suffer from any congestion which would cause you to not be able to breathe easily though the nose, just shift to your mouth. Open your lips slightly, gently blowing out, and gently drawing breath in. Pay attention to the sensation of air moving across your lips, rather than your nose. However, the result is exactly the same.

One moment, there will be nothing but the breath, and the next moment, there will just be nothing. You will have shut off your outside world, and are successfully meditating. This may open you to some experiences within the Force, but more often than not, it does not. That is because this first step in meditation is meant to break the ego from the experience. You are sitting, silent and still, with just yourself.

Over the years, I have seen people employ this same type of focus, but in different ways. Some people focus on where the tips of their pointer fingers make contact with the rest of their hand folded into itself. Others will cup their hands together in a more traditional position and focus on either where their thumbs touch, or the empty hollow of their cupped palms. This second one is seen in the mythos at the beginning of Episode Six, as the freshly-realized Knight enters the picture for the first time. Of the various hand positions, I personally prefer this one, because it reminds me of the In-yo presented at the beginning of each chapter.

However you feel most comfortable, everyone should take the time to get good at this step before moving to any of the more advanced meditations, because holding this level of intentional disconnect is essential for any of the meditation techniques taught hereafter.

There are three primary forms of meditations that are practiced in the teachings of the Force. They are **Void**, **Moving**, and **Celestial**. Some of the skills of one set will appear in the practice of others, such as the principles of Void meditation can be found in some forms of Moving meditation, such as the Active Void meditation presented further in this section.

The reason that we classify these different types is because of their intended goals. Once we know the goal of a particular form of meditation, it makes it easier to modify them for our individual benefit, or to create new meditation frameworks to better aid us in reaching a particular result from the practice. That is to say that while there are several forms of meditation presented in this section, they are not all that can be done. In my time practicing the teachings of the Force, I have run across a vast multitude of variations of meditation, but they all typically fall within the framework of Void, Moving, or Celestial. There are the occasional oddities, but those are very particular, and specialized practices that are beyond the scope of this work.

Void meditation is designed to find that moment of total disconnect, total stillness and emptiness. The beginner breathing meditation that we just covered is a simplified Void meditation, but it is used as a preparation for deeper trance states, so it is offered separately. The most commonly known type of this meditation is the Japanese practice of Zazen.

Moving meditation is often not moving mindlessly. It is instead moving with a state of refined awareness, and of total openness to what is moving around you, as you move within it.

Celestial meditation is a very wide group of practices, but they are all rooted in one primary goal: increased connection and resonance with the Force. This is where we find the totality of the mystery, and glimpse the vast complexity of the Infinite and Unknown. This is when we come to truly understand that we are just the subjective vessel of the objective All. I know these words sound a bit vague, and maybe a bit wistful, but it is not simple putting into words a description of something of such magnitude.

Enough of the prefacing, let's get started. These meditation exercises are presented by their overall execution, rather than a step-by-step explanation. Getting too detailed in instruction kills the fluidity of the experience, so let the instructions settle into your mind, and do what feels correct. Also, keep in mind that some of these meditation frameworks will take time to do correctly. One of the biggest problems with today's society is that we expect things far too quickly. This is not something that you can just expect to master in a night. Let it take time, and enjoy the process of a subtle shifting, rather than having to adjust to some over-paced expectation.

Seated Void

Framework: Void
Difficulty: Beginner

This meditation is intended to find the silent point of the mind, where we exist outside of time and space. It is achieved through repeated practice, and often involves putting the body in an uncomfortable position, though not one that will cause any injury, such as full lotus position. Shaolin have been known to teach this while doing deep splits, or long-held stances. Advanced Zazen traditions often include someone striking your back, to hone your focus.

From this point, the trick is focusing on the sensation of just one thing that does not cause discomfort, to the exclusion of all other sensations. Once there, let that single point slip away as well, and find the emptiness of the mind. It will come and go, but with practice, this state can be held for extended lengths of time, but feel like an instant. This type of practice, when combined with martial arts training, has been shown to increase physical awareness, internal and external, as well as overall control of movement (or intentional stillness).

Golden Light/Smoke

Framework: Void
Difficulty: Beginner

This exercise is where we find that empty state in our mind by focusing on a single visual. See yourself seated, and your body is a clear vessel, filled with black smoke. That smoke is all of the stress, irritation, pain, or anything else that you want to cleanse yourself of. Now, see that smoke-filled vessel floating in golden light. With each breath in, pull in that golden light, and breathe out that black smoke. See how with each breath, the smoke slowly begins to get lighter, and as you breathe out, see the smoke dissipate into the golden light, until it is gone. Do this for as long as it takes to fill the vessel with the golden light so much that you can barely see the clear vessel. Reaching that point is the first goal of this exercise, but feel free to hold that for as long as you can.

Active Void

Framework: Void
Difficulty: Intermediate

This is similar to the Seated Void in end result but the process is a bit different. First, being able to consistently reach a state of Seated Void will be a great help to this exercise. Rather than being stationary, or in discomfort, this technique grows out of a skill that you have mastered to the point that you no longer have to think about the action. Such as a simple physical skill, like moving a bag from one place to another, over and over, for hours. The mind will turn off its consciousness, and let this simple skill run on reflex. The goal is to learn how to enter that flow at will, so that your mind no longer decides to move with an action. This is often found in long time practitioners of the martial arts, when performing technique or forms, where they will slip out of their active mind, and everything will just flow.

Walking Meditation

Framework: Moving
Difficulty: Beginner

The practice of walking meditation is one that can be a bit difficult to get into, but that is because of the way we are programmed to study things quickly, and dismiss them if they are of no benefit. Walking meditation helps to bring us into a more complete connection with the world around us as we move through it. It is a simple process, but it will grow in intensity as you move further on your Path. First, begin by going for a walk in a natural place, such as a park or the woods. Have no set destination, and no serious time limit, and just walk. Pay attention to every step.

Feel the foliage as it gives way under your feet. Be mindful that you are stepping into the habitat of countless small things, like insects and worms, that help to maintain the ecosystem...

so step lightly. Strive to reach out with your internal senses, into the Force around you. Feel the cycles, feel the living energy as it flows around you. Feel the ebb and flow, the waxing and waning of the energy. Feel this at dawn, or dusk, if possible.

Step with the Force, in the Force, as the Force. Feel the Force flow from the soles of your feet into the earth with each step. Do this barefoot, if possible. Feel the connection to nature, to the world. We do not come from cities. We come from the ocean, from the forest, from the rivers, from the mountains. We are life, and we come from the living world. See the Living in all things, big and small. See the family unit of the birds in their nest, and the predatory cycle of the hawk to the mice. See the dynamic shifting of the balance, and realize that the Force is ever-moving, always flowing. Balance is a dance, not a stance.

Mantras

Framework: Moving
Difficulty: Intermediate

Mantras are a unique type of chanting that are used to create a meditative state, most commonly a void state, but not always. They are usually done stationary, but because they involve the active chanting, this qualifies as more of a Moving meditation. As was mentioned in the previous section on Practices, a Force follower already has a mantra that they can use in meditation, the Guardian's Mantra. It was explained from a point of philosophical and spiritual teaching in that section, but when we see it as a true meditative practice, we find another benefit of it. Mantras are words of phrases that are chanted, repeated over and again. This shifts the mind to the sole focus of the meaning of the word or phrase being used, as well as the disconnect caused by being able to act mindlessly. We distract the ego by giving it a task, in this case repeating the chant endlessly, and then we can step away from it with part of our mind, and access the Force more intuitively, and intimately.

Mantras have been used throughout history, and can be seen as the earliest forms of affirmations. Nearly all examples of mantras come from Eastern spiritual studies, and while they may mean something deep and spiritual to those who use them around the world, knowing the meaning of the words changes the impact they hold, even more so if fluent in the native language. Look at what is likely the most famous of traditional mantras:

Om Mani Padme Aum

This is a chant that is used to create a hypnotic tone and tempo in its repeated evocation, and it does a fantastic job of that. It helps to alter the brainwaves, but at the same time, it reinforces the meaning in the mind, once you learn it. The following is a very stylized translation of this mantra. There are more simplified translations, but I chose this version because it offers a more expressive look at the practice.

Essence of the five bodies and five wisdoms, the one with jewel and lotus, please protect the six classes of beings from their suffering!

Quite a mouthful, isn't it? That is another benefit of mantras, reinforcing complex ideas in the mind using a more distilled approach. Having a small group of sounds convey such deep meaning, once we know that meaning, is of amazing benefit to the practice.

However, not *all* mantras come from the East. My first exposure to a mantra used to focus the mind to work in the Force was in the movie *Excalibur*, with Merlin's spell chant that he used for all of his work, called the Charm of Making

**An'nal Nath'rach
O'orth Vhasis Beth'ad
Do'shen Di'enve**.

This charm has roots in old Gaelic, and has

been adopted by many Celtic restoration and Neopagan groups as a viable mantra, because it invokes a certain focus, reinforced by the imagery associated with it. It also has an interesting translation, but one that holds far less impact on the mind than the actual chant itself. The imagery is impactful nonetheless.

Breath of the serpent, spell of death and life, your song of making.

This goes to show that one can find mantras in any number of places. It all depends on where you look, and if the words resonate with your intention and spirit. Do not be afraid to adopt any mantras to your practice, so long as they are aligned with the intention of the harmonious balance of the Ashla.

Some practitioners of the meditative arts also develop their own mantras, which can be of intense personal impact. Also, the use of a single sound can be used, such as the solitary use of the *Om* in meditative practice. Explore, research, and see what fits best for you. The

Way of the Force is open to anything that came before it, and even that which can come after it. The Force is, after all, ever-moving, and ever-changing. Our practices can adapt and adopt, along the way. In time, there may even be some mantras specific to the Forcist Way, but this has not come to pass yet.

Mudras

Framework: Moving
Difficulty: Advanced

The practice of mudras also comes from the East. They are finger-weaving exercises used to focus the mind towards a particular point of intention, or towards a certain state of mental readiness. Some say that the weaving of the fingers creates particular patterns in the energy gateways in the hands that help to generate these particular mind states, others feel that the response is a trained one, but neither can be proven definitively, so make your own assumptions, and dive into the practice, but always be willing for time and exposure to change those assumptions, rather than set them into dogma.

Most modern magick practitioners use the same principle for their castings, either small or during high ritual. They are often referred to in this respect as triggers, as you train the mind that a particular position of the hand triggers a response in the subconscious mind. Similar to the crossed fingers as a sign to ward against bad luck. Catholicism often uses the sign of the cross to ward off bad luck and evil spirits, as well.

The Forcist uses these types of training exercises to help as well. Within the mythos, one can often see an extension of the hand as a projection of the Force. A wave may be used to blur the mind of the unsuspecting, the open hand extended often calls for a wave of Force energy, both for offensive and defensive application.

As the mythos also shows us, with enough training and practice, these methods are not needed, even when they prove to be of great aid. The point of this practice is not to become dependent of the hand motion, but rather to use the hand motion to train the mind and spirit to quickly be ready to call for the Force in any number of ways.

Outside of the mythos, another place to see this practice displayed to a sensational extent is the older ninja movies from the 1960s and 1970s. The practice, in traditional ninja training, is called Kuji-in, and is a distinct set of nine mudras used in deep, advanced meditative training. While finding these mudras, and some level of explanation as to what they do, is relatively easy in the digital age, in depth training is often reserved for the advanced instructor and master ranks in many ninjutsu systems, so their applied exposure beyond the old movies is a bit rare. However, the practice stems from older, more complex Buddhist practices.

As this is not a text meant to convey such a complex topic, the specifics of the Buddhist mudras will be left to each of you to dig deeper into, should you feel the need. However, the use of hand gestures as triggers is relatively easily discussed, so let's get to that.

Begin by choosing a simple hand gesture.

Make it something easy to do with one hand, quickly, and discretely. However, also be sure that it is not something you do in your daily life. For example, if you are prone to giving a thumbs up as a positive non-verbal response, that will make turning it into a trained trigger much more difficult, and far less practical. We want to be sure that we always move with intent, so that the action is successful.

When I began training these, I used to use a double tap of the right thumb to my right middle finger. It is small, often unnoticed, and not something that I would otherwise typically do. I chose my right hand because I was training to reflexively extend energy, and as I am right-handed, using my projecting hand, or Power Hand, was the most logical choice.

Once you have that simple gesture decided, put yourself in a meditative state, and focus on calling up the subconscious alteration that you want to program. For the sake of this exercise, let's say that you are training a trigger to quickly open your senses to the area around you. So, you would open your senses as far as you can, and do your gesture. Hold that state, and do your gesture again.

Repeat this as many times as you can, with a small pause between each time. The second that your senses slip, and shut down, stop doing the gesture. Practice this for one to three weeks before ever attempting to use the gesture to cause the change in focus. Just like learning to write: the skill may come instantly now, but we all struggled with it at the beginning. If it does not work right away, just realize that you have to train your mind to do new things slowly, and do not allow yourself to keep attempting the trigger as you get more frustrated. That frustration will build barriers in your mind that will only slow down the process of learning and growing into your skills, and connection to the Force. Remember, to doubt one's self does only to ensure those doubts.

Inner Temple

Framework: Celestial
Difficulty: Beginner

This meditation exercise will make the first of the celestial framework meditations. When we talk about the celestial framework, let us keep in mind that these are exercises and practices of deep spiritual impact. The benefits come from the doing, and the changes that come from the repeated doing. These techniques are not meant to bring about a simple change, but rather something that alters the spirit, and how the Forcist interacts with the Force, and the world around them. These are the most direct form of spiritual alchemy that anyone can take part in.

To begin this more personal and transformative part of one's training, let us first start by building a safe haven for our recovery, because these practices can get to be a bit intense. In this place, we can review what we learn in our deeper meditative practices. Sometimes called the Inner Keep, or the Inner Sanctum, we like to refer to this as the Inner Temple.

The difference in name is a bit intentional. A Keep, a Sanctum, a Castle: these things all breed an image of high walls, of impenetrable defenses, and of a sense of retreat. Sometimes, there is need to retreat. We will find, in our deeper training, parts of who we are that are unpleasant, and difficult to assimilate into our spiritual evolution.

The image of a Temple, on the other hand, still offers that subconscious sense of safety, but as a place of learning and growth, rather than just retreat and healing. Healing from a hard lesson is important, but so too is the importance of learning the lesson. We don't want to make a habit of running and hiding because a situation becomes overwhelming. Instead, we want to build a better reaction. We want to step back into a place of centered connection, so that we can review what has brought us to that point, and pull from it what lessons there are to learn at that time.

Let's enter into a state of centered connection, and find ourselves in what many new age spiritual practices called the White Room. This is an empty, endless expanse of pure white, and pure manifestation. Envision the Construct, the loading program from the *Matrix* franchise, where things are best illustrated, where lessons are taught, and where the tools for dealing with the coming experiences can be brought to you. The White Room is a place between the conscious and the subconscious, between the mind and the Force. It exists in time, and outside of time. Because of its infinitely malleable nature, some even feel that this is the place where dreams take form. Take as long as you need to reach this place. It may take moments, it may take months. Remember, this road is one without end, and so we must allow ourselves the time to grow into our new place in the Force. Take the time, as you need it.

Once you have the White Room, manifest in it, a door. This door will change throughout your life, so do not be concerned if it is different from one day to the next. Behind this door, know that there is a place that is totally safe, a place that will help you to open yourself to what you are having a difficult time processing. When ready, open this door and walk into it.

On the other side of that room, you will find what you feel is the most supportive and nurturing surroundings for what you need to do. No two people will ever have the same Inner Temple. I have one friend who sees the inner courtyard of an older medieval home. Another friend often finds himself in a beautiful garden, with a stream, a cool breeze, and a gently warming sun. Because of my training, I typically walk into either a richly cushioned meditation room, or a larger version of my home dojo. When I was a younger man, this usually took the form of a mountain range with a raging storm in the distance, as I have always had a sense of awe for the power of nature unleashed.

Whatever form this room takes, know that it is always a part of you, a room always ready for you should it be needed. The longer that you stay inside your Inner Temple, the more solid parts of it will become. It will also begin to take the same flowing characteristics as the White Room, in the shifting nature of time and manifestation that can be done here. Be sure to make note of what changes when you enter the Inner Temple each time. You can make changes rather easily, but what is there when you first come in, should it be noticeably out of the ordinary, is often important.

Sometimes, you will even see other people in your Inner Temple, but you should never be concerned about this. This is a place of you, inside of you. Anyone that appears there is either a being that has a strong, positive connection to you, or is a manifestation of the spirit, and it comes bearing lessons to be learned.

Remember, this is a place of learning and

processing, not a place to hide from the world, or from the problems that you may be facing in your life, or on your spiritual journey. Abusing this safe haven can stunt any development you make along the Way. The Force follower is bold, and should treat their Path the same way. Do not let yourself get beat down, but do not retreat due to a simple lump on the ego, or bump in the road.

Shrinking

Framework: Celestial
Difficulty: Intermediate

The Shrinking meditation is the second of the celestial meditations that we are going to begin with. The end result of this meditation is very similar to that of the Growing meditation, which is presented after this one, but this one aligns better with the practices of Void meditation as a start.

Before beginning this training, it is recommended that you get some way to document experiences, because looking at the levels below what we are used to seeing can be enlightening, or even a bit jarring. It can be spoken recordings, or a notebook and pen. Just be sure that you have them handy as you begin this practice, even if you don't use them. You do not want to lament not having them later. Each of the following steps, while explained somewhat quickly, may take a long time to reach, to process, or to move beyond. Records of your experiences may be needed to show growth that you may not see in the moment.

To begin, we must be mindful of where we are in the life cycle. We exist in a state at the edge of the Living and the Guiding. We must start this journey at the highest point of the Living, a point of flowing vibrance, interwoven with all living things, the edges of our Forceform glowing with a brilliant golden light.

The next step is to collapse our Forceform into itself, making our presence denser, but smaller. Then, we must do so again, and again. Continue to collapse into your Forceform until you lose the definition of the Living, and are swimming in the turbulence and flow of the Dynamic.

Hold this point, an active part of all things, but nothing holding shape or definition. Allow it to make an impression on your spirit. Feel it move through you, around you, and past you, like being at the bottom of a deep river. Feel what lessons it has to remind you of. For a time, this is as far as you will be able to shrink, but it goes further.

Once comfortable in this state, be that moments or months later, shrink the Forceform even further. Collapse it into a dense, hard shell of just yourself. Feel the spark of the Force in you, that is all of what makes you who you are. Feel that unique vibration in the Force that you see in your eyes when you stare into the mirror. That is the Internal, something many martial traditions refer to as the One Point. It is at this point that you are pure in your connection with yourself, and how that changes the Force as it flows into you, and out through you.

Grow as comfortable here as you can, but the journey is not yet done. Remember, we are all just the subjective expression of the objective All. As such, we are connected to that All, like a strand of hair running back to the scalp.

Once you are comfortable in the Internal, turn even further into it. Shrink your Forceform even more totally. Feel the collapse, minute and infinite at the same time. Become the energy of the Force, as it travels on the beam of light that is your divine spark. Keep pushing into the sensation, smaller and smaller, until you lose all sense of yourself. Follow that spark back to the origin of all things, the Force.

Once that point is reached, many have stated that they felt as if their essence exploded out into the whole of the universe, and by losing hold of the sense of self, they found themselves experiencing the All, the Force in its purest form: the Infinite and Unknown. Some have stated to see flowing patterns, others have experienced the "heartbeat of the universe". It is not uncommon to hear what I call the echo of creation.

Don't be discouraged if you cannot reach this point right away. There are some people who, due to their past, do not do well with the idea of shrinking their sense of self to nothing right away, and that can be a bit of a hindrance in this exercise. However, once that state is reached through other means, coming back to this practice can be of great benefit. Live here as long as you can. Be outside of your sense of self, and experience the rawest nature of all things. Be elated, be numb, be whole, and be empty.

Growing

Framework: Celestial
Difficulty: Intermediate

As was mentioned, the Growing meditation is very similar in end result, but the method is different. This one is a slight bit more difficult because, rather than diminishing the sense of self, we are expanding it, which can cause a bit of an ego trip the first few times. However, this is the second side of the same coin, and should not be neglected in our training, either. This method forces us to push our limits harder into realms of our spiritual being that we are maybe not ready for yet, or even understand, so take this slowly.

As with the Shrinking meditation, it is strongly recommended that you have on hand some way to document the experiences of stepping from one level of connection to the Force to the next in such an intense way. Again, do not rush this process. Grow into it naturally, and you will get far more from it. As mentioned, this side of the practice can cause some ego tripping. By that, I don't mean a spike of superiority, but rather that the sense of self is being stretched further than it is ready for, so the ego will hide from what it may be experiencing, and you may fall into a false step along the way. Just be mindful, and if the situation seems almost too easy, it probably isn't the right step. However, you know you better than anyone. Trust what you feel is right, even if proven later to be wrong. You may have needed the trip with your ego.

First, we once again find ourselves at the edge of the Living and the Guiding, a beacon of pure light, radiating out into the world around us, and into the flow of the Force itself. Once we comfortably find that state, we begin to expand out into the Force, breaking the boundaries of our physical form, and becoming more aligned with the Guiding. We become a more active component in the flow of the Force, both moving with it and moving it with us.

That is the first step, the first level of Growing. It is a powerful experience, and the first time can be a bit overwhelming. Take as much time as you need to grow more comfortable with this state. Feel the very airy nature of the Force as it moves around you and through you. It is the flow, the pattern of life. Bask in it, and allow your connection to become more comfortable with this ever-moving current of life.

Once you are truly comfortable in this state, no matter how long it takes, only then do we want to move further into this practice. Once ready, raise your energy even further, expand out into the limitlessness, and take hold of the web of all things, the Uniting. Feel the inter-connectivity to a depth beyond what many have ever experienced. Become one with everything, become that vastness, that wholeness, the web of Everything. Once again, be here as long as you need to be.

Once ready, push further, larger. Feel the fabric of space and time, the flexing, shifting, crystalline structure of the entire universe. Flow in the vastness of the Cosmic, and feel it as it stretches your mind and understanding. Swim in this startlingly complex simplicity of it all. Become the contradiction that is being both finite and endless, subjective and objective. Whereas in the Uniting, you become the web of all, the Cosmic is what is between each strand of the web. It is the darkness between the stars, where the true nature of all things lie, dormant and invisible to the uninitiated.

This one is a harder point to move beyond, but keep reaching. Reach out so far that you feel your essence dissipate, like mist in the morning sun, as it wafts away into non-existence. Feel the boundaries that are your sense of self as it fades into the Infinite and Unknown, just as with the Shrinking meditation before.

Some people might wonder why they should have to train both forms of this, if the end result is the same: the Infinite and Unknown, but the answer is in the concern. Our experience of the energy of all things is limited to where we are.

The Force exists in a state before us, and in a state beyond us. While both points reach the Infinite, each end is a different form of the Unknown. Think infrared and ultraviolet light. Both exist outside of our ability to see, but they are two very different things, used in very different ways, once we learned how to harness them. What is to say that, some day, we will not develop an even greater understanding of the Force beyond the Cosmic, and below the Internal... but in doing so, we learn that these new phases are very different in their characteristics? We cannot lock ourselves away from any form of enlightenment just to make the training easier, or stay locked into some dogmatic breakdown of what we cannot fully understand.

Remember, this is not a practice that a beginner can typically get to in an afternoon. The steps will come, and they will each make their impact on the student. Do not think that you have to be able to reach any point any time soon. The Way of the Force is a lifelong pursuit. Let it grow with you, and enrich every day.

Astral Temple/Akashic Records

Framework: Celestial
Difficulty: Advanced

There is, within the Cosmic vibration of the Force, a depository of all knowledge. It is known in many esoteric and occult schools as the Akashic Records. Some groups also call this place the Astral Temple. For our purposes, the two terms will be synonymous, and will be used interchangeably. In order to reach this place, though, we must first begin with breaking the bonds of the physical experience, and begin your introduction to the Astral Plane.

There are many different methods for reaching the Astral Plane, but we are going to start with one of the simplest, and most direct techniques I have ever seen work. As always, we must start in a state of harmonious balance with the Force, and the world around us. The first step is to cause an out of body experience. We do that by focusing on the flow of blood in the body, as it courses with each beat of the heart. After we can feel that steady rhythm, feel deeper, and feel the way the Force circulates through your Forceform. Its flow will initially match that of the flow of the blood. However, we can change the flow of the Forceform: speed it up, slow it down, make it higher pressure, make it a mere trickle. Practice this step as long as you need to.

Once you can control the flow in the Forceform, let that flow build an image in your mind's eye of the Forceform, overlaying the physical body as you meditate. Now, lift the arm of your Forceform without lifting your physical arm. The first time you do this may be difficult. You may even feel the muscles in your physical arm twitch, as if initiating movement. That is perfectly normal. Our entire lives have been spent directing energy by way of directing the physical self. If you wanted to pick something up, you would not spend hours attempting to draw it to you with just your mind. You would direct your energy into your limbs to perform the action.

However, with practice, you will be able to remove the movements of your Forceform from your physical form. I have never met anyone who could not do this, given enough time and focus.

Once you can pull your Forceform from your body, you will be having what most people call an out of body experience, or OBE. Much can be learned in this state, most specifically about your self image, and where that needs work. However, once you are having this OBE, you can also gain some interesting connections to life forms around you, both of this plane and of the Otherworld. It is not uncommon to interact with a spirit guide or nature spirit in this state.

OBEs are technically a form of astral projection, but that alone will not get us to the Astral Temple. We just have to be in a position where we can easily go into an OBE state to better access it. If you have no experience with this, please don't expect to get this technique in a day or two. Just training the mind to divorce the Forceform from the body can take months, so don't rush it, and don't get discouraged if you don't get this right away.

Once you are ready, you have to enter into a meditative state, and follow a variation of the Growing meditation described previously. However, you are taking your Forceform, is as solid as you can keep it, to the Cosmic. It is here that you will experience the Astral Temple.

Reaching the Cosmic is reaching the Astral Plane. Being here is difficult to get to, but it is an amazing place to be. Time alters in ways that are beyond words, and manifestation is even more instant and powerful than the White Room or the Inner Temple. Here, you will encounter countless forms of life. Spirit guides may find you here, but so too will Otherworldly beings. There are even some beings on the Plane that could be considered deities. All things that we can experience in the Force exist here.

Once you can reach the Cosmic with your Forceform, look for a structure. Some see a giant library, some see a mountain cave, some see a small building with a pillar of light coming from the top. Make your way to that building. Once you are there, send out a request for entry. It doesn't need to be words, but it can be, if that is what the Force calls for you to do.

Finding the Akashic Records is a fantastically difficult thing, especially if you are new to any form of deep spiritual training. Finding them does not guarantee entry, either. When you are able to find it, you are very close to being ready to enter, but if there is any flow in your intention, then the way may stay blocked. Do not be disheartened by that, however. We are all imperfect beings, on a journey to become more at one with the Force. When the time is right, the doors will open, and even once they do, there will be sections of the information that you will not be allowed right away, or perhaps ever. I know that I have not seen all of its mysteries, yet.

As a warning, be mindful of the Astral Plane. As mentioned, there are countless other forms of life in this place, and the ability to create is almost instant. Just as there are predators in the mundane world, there are similar predators within the Astral. Most of them, however, are not drawn into spiritual warfare for no reason. As with all life, treat anything you encounter with respect, and you should have little issue. However, because it is a possibility, do not explore the Astral Plane too deeply before learning the Shielding skill, presented in the next section.

Exercises & Training

The Reason We Train

We have spoken at some length about our connection to the Force, our alignment with the All, and how we can grow more attuned to it. There are several mediation frameworks listed in this book, with countless more available, should a person either look to the wider world, or strive to create one of their own. These meditations are the first step in what the Forcist often calls "Forcework", or more commonly "training".

We, as living beings, exist in the Force in a constant shift between one of two states: passive practice and active practice.

Passive practice is when we train to look into

ourselves, and apply the Force to better grow as people, and to heal the injuries we have sustained along the way, in the body, in the mind, and in the spirit. Active practice is pushing further into the Force, and jumping into the flow of the Force, allowing it to take you where it can go. It is in this type of practice that we learn just how much we really are one with the Force. This training opens us to feats and skills on par with the feats of the mythos, the wizards of legend, and the spiritual masters of the Eastern world.

Neither type of training is superior to the other, because each requires some level of give and take. You give of your time for your training, and when you do not have large chunks of time for training, then you will not be able to easily access some of the active practices. However, that may simply be because the flow of the Force needed you somewhere else. The Force comes to each of us in our own unique ways, and no one person will be able to do everything all the time. The point isn't to become some kind of *super psychic mojo master*, either. It is to become more fully one with the Force as it exists in you, and with you.

Passive Training

Passive Practice makes up the majority of most training in the Force. That is because we either do not need the greater, more active skills, or because they are not as fully understood and developed by those who offer direct training to others. That is acceptable, because most often, we are not called to act in grand ways, but rather to act in subtle ways. The subtle nature of these callings should never be taken as a point of inconsequence. It is the subtle things that allow for all of the greater actions to come into being.

When we learn to move around freely, we must first build the strength to stand up, and then gain the understanding of our equilibrium to stay on our feet. From there, we build strength until we can put all of our weight on one leg, so that we can take our first wobbly steps. Even then, we have to keep working on our balance, because strength alone will not keep our weak and uncertain legs beneath us.

Each of those small, subtle things are required to learn how to walk, let alone run. So, give yourself time. Don't try to run right out of the gate because you just started standing up on your own.

Sensing

The practice of Sensing is a very broad topic, but it can truly be distilled to a small collection of training exercises which, with practice, can be experimented with so that you can better discover the depth of your own connection and ability. Sensing is also one of the primary skills needed to create any impact in the Force, passive or active. If you are blind to what is going on around you, then there is no way that you can effect consistent change.

There are a few different types of sensing, but they mostly work off of the same basic principle. Some of those types are as follows:

- Presence
- Negative Presence
- Motion
- Distortion/Disturbance
- Reflection
- Emotional Outburst

◆ Focused Intention

These are some of the more common ways that a person can sense what is going on around them. They all hinge, however, on the ability to feel one's surroundings through the Force. Within the mythos, this was always described as reaching out with your feelings, but even that can be a bit too vague. So, we have to start by teaching what exactly you are supposed to be feeling.

I want to go ahead and remind everyone: these are long-term training exercises. You might be able to do them in with a day or two's practice, but most often, even the beginning steps take months of trial and error before success is found. So, be generous with yourself, give the time needed to fail, regroup, and try again.

Begin this practice in a closed room. Somewhere familiar to you, where you can relax and be undisturbed for a length of time.

Get into a relaxed state, and just observe the room. Let's say that this is your bedroom, or home office. You know where everything in the room is because it is familiar to you. Now, look at an item in the room, such as a statue on a bookshelf. Envision yourself holding that item, feeling its shape, its texture, and its weight. This is something that you are familiar with enough that, if there were duplicates of the item, you would be able to know which one was yours from the other.

Now, expand that sensation. Feel where it rests on the shelves, and then take in the whole shelf. Then the books on the shelf. Then the floor. Let that expand across the whole floor, and up the walls, to the ceiling. Feel the entire structure of the room, as if mapping it for a digital model. Once you have that feeling, close your eyes.

The first few times that you do this, the second you close your eyes, you will lose the focus and clarity of the room, but that is okay. Just push yourself back out into the room around you.

Feel the corners of the walls, and the edges of the floor and ceiling. Feel the box in which you currently reside.

Once you can feel the room, begin to reintroduce some of the surrounding items to the framework. Build the most complete picture that you can. Be gentle, and open yourself more fully to the Force around you. As your connection to the Force grows, so too will the clarity of your initial senses. As these senses grow, you will find that the other forms of sensing tend to grow naturally. You will feel currents of energy shifting around you. You will begin to know when someone is approaching you, even to the precision of knowing who. You will even be able to feel emptiness in the Force around you, which often signified a being, corporeal or astral, not wanting to be noticed. This type of sensation can be casual, or intentional, by reaching out in all directions, to find the void.

You will also gain a level of sensing the energy of the land around you. You may feel the revelry of a recent festival, or the pain of a long-forgotten battle. The Force is bent by the outbursts of emotion that come about in grand occasions.

Emotional energy from other people will become clearer, which can be a bit overwhelming in the beginning. With enough practice, you will learn the difference between your emotional energy, and that of other people, but we will discuss how to deal with those energies more directly next, with an equally important skill.

Shielding

The Force is a vast and powerful thing, and once we open ourselves to it, especially at first, it can be a bit overwhelming. It would be like opening your eyes for the first time, and seeing the sun in all its brilliance. It is beautiful, and comforting, but it can also burn both the eyes and the skin. When we go out into an extremely bright day, humans have created many things to aid us in experiencing the sunny day without the discomfort it can cause, such as large brimmed hats, and sunglasses.

As we take our first steps into the power and density of the Force, the Forcist has developed skills to It is a way to block out energy from the Force, in part or in full. Up to this point, we have discussed methods to open ourselves to the Force, but there are several reasons that one may need to close that connection down. Let's look at a few

- ◆ Empathic Overload
- ◆ Energetic Interference
- ◆ Energetic Attack, Local or Otherworldly
- ◆ Negative Energy Echo
- ◆ Negative Presence
- ◆ Akashic Overload
- ◆ Forceform Disruption

There are many other reasons why we could employ a shielding technique of some kind, but I am pretty sure that this list makes a good enough example for now. The important thing to remember is that a shield is not just something that a person needs for any form of energetic attack. There are some schools of new age practice that do not teach shielding, and others who see it as a tool of spiritual warfare, but just like sunglasses, the skill is simply there to keep a person safe from spiritual injury.

This skillset is all built on a very simple and direct technique. You feel deep into yourself, and touch on your Internal vibration of the Force, that solid point of just yourself at the center of the Base Gateway. Once you have hold of that, you draw that ball out into a sphere around your entire Forceform, keeping it as solid a shell as you can. Once you have that shell, make it thicker, and denser, until you are no longer bothered by the energy towards you.

As with any defensive skill, this can be a bit difficult to test, as it requires putting yourself in a state of energetic stress, or under direct spiritual assault, in order to test it. That is why it is more important that you train yourself to extend this bubble around you quickly, and efficiently. When training, make the shield dense enough to shut out the "psychic static" from the area around you.

Be sure to experiment with different manifestations of these bubbles. Different densities, different shapes, different points of isolation, even different colors. Learn the difference in a solid chrome box, a flowing wall of spiritual fire, and a semi-clear pink bubble. The method of manifestation will depend greatly on both the energy you are trying to block yourself against, and you as a person.

Toy with being sensitive to the movements of life around you, and then closing it all out. Going shopping during busy hours is a fantastic place to test these skills safely, as you develop them to be fast enough that you can raise a shield while doing other things.

The most important part of this is that, as you learn to look beyond the physical, and see beyond just your eyes, your presence will undoubtedly be noticed by things that exist on different planes, different vibrations of the Force. These things may become curious, and they may come to see who and what you are. Most often, these things do not mean you any harm, but their presence in your sphere may cause a great deal of anxiety, or discomfort. Tossing up a shield is usually enough to back those things off, as they then see that you were aware of them, and make them uncomfortable by their presence. That is not to say that it will work every time, but more things in existence are far more curious than malicious.

Self Healing

The Force is the *prima materia*, the fabric of all things. As such, it has the potential to do limitless good, or limitless harm. The Forcist is not one who seeks to do harm, because to harm another person is to harm another subjective avatar of the Force, just as they are. To harm another is to harm the self, and to bring imbalance to the Force.

However, the Force is that which brings life, and through it, it gives the Force follower the ability to heal. The body already does this, naturally. We are only talking about ways to make that a faster, and more efficient process.

There are several well-documented cases over the years of phenomena that are attributed to "power of prayer" and "faith healing". These are not any different from what we are discussing, except that we take more intrinsic responsibility for the action, rather than masking it as a gift that we were only offered because we asked enough times.

That wording seems a bit harsh, but it wasn't meant to. The mainstream religions that lean on faith healing have just as much right to their spiritual practices as anyone else, but one thing they do is they send out their desire for health, and then wash their hands of the responsibility thereof. They put it in the hands of their higher power. This becomes a point of failure for those who may not have a true connection to the All, or who doubt the ability for such things to become true. That is the reason that this discussion is happening this late in this book. If you have been undertaking the meditations and exercises up to this point, you will likely be beyond a limiting level of doubt. The Force teaches us one very important lesson:

To doubt one's self does only to ensure those doubts.

This statement is one I have echoed for decades, and it still acts as a mantra of self-reflection for me, as well as a bolster to act, at times. When we work with the Force in a way that should bring about results, doubt is the weak point in the chain, and can be stressed to a break with little more than a few moments of fear. Be mindful.

Now that we have the underlying principle covered, let's look at how we can use the Force to heal ourselves. First, as was already mentioned, this is not meant to take the place of the natural immune system. Forcists are not arrogant enough to believe that we know how to make this biomechanical machine work better than its design. Instead, we use the Force to amplify the process. Sometimes, that means to reinforce the potency of a white blood cell. Other times, it can be to ease the release of certain chemicals, such as endorphins, to ease pain. With enough practice, there are even times where we can stimulate these chemicals in higher doses than normal.

There are times that our immune system needs help from outside of our body, and in cases like that, we can use the Force to help any outside medicines to work better, or last longer, or even mitigate side-effects, such as blood pressure spikes, or dizziness. I have even had students tell me that their connection to the Force can help to dull the pain of a chronic condition as well as any medication, sometimes more so.

To do this, we must first learn how our body feels in a healthy state, or at least as healthy as possible. When we do not have that feeling already, we can do a comparison. For example, let's say that I twisted my ankle wrong, and caused nerve irritation. That irritation isn't too bad, but because I am not favoring that ankle, my stride changes, and is all the way into my lower back.

In this case, I can use the Force in my hands to help massage away any built up pressure, or energy blockages, by comparing the Force flow in my right side to that of my uninjured left side. A laying meditation can also be employed, using the ability to disconnect the Forceform from the physical body to help to realign the flow, and remove what pain can be released.

Using the OBE techniques discussed before, we can even pull our Forceform out, and see any energy blockages in it directly, and help to correct them before we reunite with the body. This is more helpful for a repeated pain, such as back pain from a hard physical profession, but it can also be used to heal the energy system in the Forceform after any type of spiritual overload, be it overwork or incomplete shielding from an outside irritation.

However, we do not have to divorce our Forceform from our physical body in order to clear energy blockages. That can be done completely consciously, but it does take a bit of sensitivity to the interruption of flow in the Forceform. Using either approach, we can also help to speed recovery from a major illness, such as a massive sinus infection, or a bad case of food poisoning. We can cleanse the Forceform of bad energy as many times as needed to help release such toxins and infections. We can also reinforce the good energy surrounding a wound, or broken bone to help them to heal more quickly.

The bottom line of this is that we know when something is wrong, and at the core of all things is the Force. There is nothing beneath it, and nothing beyond it. As such, we can help to correct when it gets out of control or out of balance. This skill has more than just a personal use, but we will discuss that application shortly. For now, we must remember, this skill is subtle, and will take lots of use to get really good at using it to great effect. That does not mean that it is not working. That simply means that you are protected by the Force enough to not need to practice it very often.

Psychometry

The Force is energy, and energy can neither be created nor destroyed, only changed. We can actually experience the echoes of changes in some items. That is the skill of psychometry, the reading of the echoes of an object's past.

Everything comes from something, and everything has been drastically altered by something, somehow. The best example of this is in a knife. Be it hand forged, or machine produced, that metal did not come out of the ground all shiny and sharp. There was a refinement process, an alchemy of a sort. That iron ore was taken to its breaking point, and beat repeatedly to remove impurities that could cause it to fail. Some have even used that example to explain the rigors of personal training. The repeated testing of limits, going further each time, until the metal has been forged into something far stronger than what it was.

That leaves a mark. Not a hammer mark, but an echo in the Force.

But, it's not done. There is still shaping, stretching, filing, hardening, tempering, and sharpening. Each is its own little impact, its own point of change. It's still not done. Polishing the blade, building the fittings and handle, making a sheath... those are all part of the creation of a knife. So, how many hands touched it?

This is where we get into the actual psychometry. Countless people harvested the ore, and surely more than one person touched all the ore used to make this blade. Even if the blade is hand forged by one blacksmith, the billet from which the blade was stretched would have several hands in it as well.

If a machine-produced blade, there was someone who loaded the billet to be shaped, and at least one other person polishing and sharpening the blade. How many people were involved in the manufacture of the fittings? What about the sheath? The observed object is changed by the act of observation, and thus, each person who makes contact with this blade leaves a little part of their soul on it, like a spiritual fingerprint.

Psychometry is being able to hold that knife, and see that process. Feel the subtle differences between the person who spent a few seconds putting the finished product in a box and the person who watched this blade be cut for half an hour, and then inspect it for another half an hour before passing it onto the polisher. One makes a very minor impact, and the other makes a more major one.

If the blade was hand forged from billet, then you are liable to get a lot of personal details filter in about the blacksmith that made that blade into what it is. It is an interesting difference to feel.

With practice, you can identify more recent contacts with an item, even down to the person who used that item. It is a type of listening that there is no definitive technique for, other than being open to it, and lots of patient practice. Many have some skill in this, even if they have never identified it as such. We have been taught to ignore the echoes we find on and in items, but it is there. Picture a toddler looking at three identical toys, one of which was hers, and the other two were not. The odds are statistically significant that the girl will choose her own toy the first time. The child hasn't been taught to ignore the energy they are feeling. They feel their own energy, and the energy of the parents that use the toy to play with them. That is also psychometry.

I have given grand examples, as I am prone to do to draw very distinct lines in my teachings, but these extreme examples hopefully give you the ability to discern for yourself when you are experiencing this type of skill, and nurture it to something beyond doubt.

Active Training

Active Practices require a bit more preparation. If you have not worked beyond the majority of your personal doubt, then these skills will be significantly more difficult to reproduce consistently. That is because their effects are not meant to be done within yourself, but rather outside of yourself.

Reaching out into the Force, using your focus to make some noticeable change can be a daunting thing, even after years of practice and training. It is a potential danger to anyone who has any craving for power over others, or any need to feed their ego. It can become like a drug if misused. As such, these skills offered are not of any severe danger of misuse, but there are many skills that the Force affords us that can be, so any training you undertake outside of these offered should be done from a place of humility, rather than hubris. Warning aside, there are times that many Forcists are called to act in a more direct, external way when dealing with the Force, and those people around them.

Distance Healing

This is one of the most important skills that you will ever learn as a Forcist. We come from a mythos heavily steeped in war, as is seen plainly in its name. However, much of the mythos was built upon the practices of monks, healers and mystics throughout human history. The Force is the base of all things, and as such, it is best served by maintaining a healthy, harmonious balance in all aspects of itself.

As we are the subjective experience of the objective All, we are each connected to one another in ways that modern science is only now becoming very slightly aware of. However, our ancient predecessors already knew this interconnection to be a true and viable medium by which to create change. We are no different than they were, just settled in a different point in time, and we have different social expectations. Healers of old were often sought after for their wisdom. Now, we have taken a far too cold approach to health. But, we have opened our eyes up to the Force, and because of that, we each know that there is another way. It is not meant to replace, but to enhance.

We have already discussed the various levels of healing the self. Healing others at a distance is very similar, but it requires just a little bit more practice with OBEs. We have to be able to project ourselves, at least to some extent, outside of our immediate area, and into the area around the person you are training to heal. The closer you are to the person, be that physically or emotionally, the easier it will be, but with practice, proximity will be of far less consequence.

There are two primary forms of distance Forcework, and those two types are the most obvious when it comes to distance healing practices. The first is known as an Extension, whereas the second is called a Visualization. Each has their strengths, and their weaknesses, and individuals are more prone to favoring one over the other.

First, we are going to look at the Extension. This is a faster form of healing. The Forcework takes less time, and it requires less effort in its construction. It is a crude pushing on another person. For example, if someone has an illness, and the Forcist can feel a bad energy flow from the person, and so they overlay a corrected flow to help expedite the healing process, that is an extension. It is quick to implement because the Forcist is putting it directly upon the other person. The results also tend to be far more immediate for the same reason. The downside is that the extension does not typically last very long, once focus is released. There is also the possibility of the other person subconsciously rejecting the help, even if they had expressed agreement to being aided. That happens most often because of the direct, aggressive nature of extensions. That isn't to say this method is more or less ethical or proper. There are times when consent cannot be offered, or would actually create problems in the process.

The other form of distance healing is Visualization. This method is more akin to the traditions of spellcasting, as is taught in other esoteric and mystery schools. When we build a visualization, we are not putting direct effort on another person right away. Instead, it is more like forming a blueprint for improved health and wellness. This method works better for healing injuries, because of the more complex nature of a physical imbalance. In this, the Forcist would build a Forceform cast of the injury, a broken leg for example. The leg would be built in this place between the Forceform of the healer, and that of the injured. Once the proper flow of healing energy is mapped out, and the other details involved in the healing such as chemical reactions, bone fusion, and other natural acts of healing; then the framework is fed as much power as possible, to make it last as long as needed, and then placed on the injury. The primary benefit of this healing method is the ability to plan more parts of the healing process, and the longevity of the action.

Both of these methods can be employed at the

same time, in some cases, so do not feel that one has to be totally divorced of the other. Practice both methods, as you can, so that should the Force call on you to act, that you are ready and able to be the child of the Ashla that we all strive to be. You may find that you are naturally better with one method over the other, which is completely natural, but be mindful not to neglect the training of both parts of this practice. There may be a day when you need both, separately or simultaneously.

Weather Influence

This skill might seem a bit self-serving, or otherwise either silly or overly dramatic, and I must confess, the idea can be a bit to wrap one's head around at first. However, the Force offers it's children gifts that many people do not understand the value of. However, this is one skill that we have all heard being used for no personal benefit, but for altruistic purposes of a larger community. In this case, I am using the example of the rain dance. This ritual was meant to focus on bringing water to crops by way of ritual dance to build energy and focus the mind. We are still using that equation, but the active components are a personal choice. Our focus and energy is gathered through the various meditative practices that we have learned up to this point.

There are two methods for refining this skill. One will work for some people, one will work for others. For some people, both will have some effect, but I have yet to find a way to guide the student as to which is better for them on the onset, so instead, we try both ways, and see where that takes us.

The first method is to learn what makes weather change: what makes rain fall, what makes winds strengthen, even what makes lightning strike. There are physical principles for each of these things, and knowing them can help some people to create them, much like the Extensions in the previous skill.

The other method takes more time, and that requires lots of personal reflection, and a great deal of time outside watching the rain, so to speak. As with all things, the pressures and fronts that cause the shifts in our weather, as they move, they create turbulence in the Force. We can train ourselves to know those feelings as they begin.

The first method is like learning to play music by first learning music theory, and how to read sheet music. The second method is learning by ear and feel, rather than worrying over proper chords or technique. These two can feed into one another, like the by ear player using what they know to read sheet music, making their expression both mental and spiritual at the same time.

So, it's great to know that something can be explained, but other than calling rain, what do these skills do? It can help to safeguard against the imbalanced fury that is at times unleashed by nature upon us surface dwellers. For example, I have friends who live in hurricane areas. Being able to help safeguard them during terrible storms is invaluable. I personally used to live in Tornado Alley, and had used this same skill to divert bad storms from making contact, and turning into a terrible nightmare for those around the city I was in.

This brings me to the most important part of this skill, and that is to not overuse it. We should not stop rain storms just because we want to go out today. The land needs its water, and the atmosphere needs to have its cycles. Even looking at something as destructive as wildfires, there are times that that type of destruction is needed to reintroduce nutrients to the land. Just as human existence has changed our global ecosystem, abuse by those who can create these changes can be just as bad, even with the best of intentions. Be mindful, as you grow more complete in the Force.

Oneness

The state of Oneness is not something that is so easy to teach, but it is of vital importance that we understand what it is, so that when we find ourselves in that state, we are not left unaware. Previously in this book, we discussed both Shrinking and Growing meditations. These types of Celestial meditations are a good primer to reaching the state of Oneness, but they are not the same time. In those meditations, we destroy our immediate grasp on the dividing line between our personal experience and the whole of the Force. What we are doing is losing our sense of self, so that we can better understand what is beneath the bluster of the ego.

Oneness is the total opposite. In a state of total Oneness, you are all of both yourself and of the Force. The line between the ego and the All is not lost. Instead, it is expanded, and becomes a perfect conduit to and from the Force. The

Forceform is a torrent of energy, swirling like a storm in a bottle. However, the Forcist is typically extremely calm, even if the experience that caused this heightened state was active or stressful.

There are some practices that call similar experiences kundalini awakenings, or spiritual ascension. Neither are wrong, but neither are totally correct, either. They are, however, linked, and one can lead to the other. These experiences can change the way a Forcist views the world, because the unrestricted flow between the self and the All opened them to levels of understanding that they never thought possible. Some people have reported changes in eye color from these experiences, changes of voice, even massive changes in physiology. I experienced one such moment that left me glowing. Now, that could have been an overstimulation of the Third Eye, or possibly a raise in vibration high enough that I was actually producing light. I cannot be sure, nor should the specifics matter, because they are parts of the experience, and have long-since made their impact. Knowing which doesn't change anything, neither now nor would have it then.

There is no set way to reach this point, and there is no guarantee for how long one will be in it. There is also no guarantee that the experience will be a good one. You may face parts of the self that are plainly disturbing to even begin to assimilate. As painful as that is, these experiences are important. If we are haunted by something that echoes in the Force around us, that echo can go out into the rest of the Force, and hinder our becoming who we are meant to be.

This is not meant to make you push for it, or to push away from it. The Force will put you where you are meant to be, kicking and screaming if need be. If you are meant to have a bad experience, know that you will benefit from it, even if it takes some time. The Force is something so far beyond our understanding that it is difficult to conceptualize how a bad experience will ever be of benefit to us, but much like the pain of physical labor and exercise, once the muscular fatigue heals, the muscle is stronger for it. Never forget that the Force does not play favorites, nor does it hold grudges. It gives what is needed to all who walk in the universe, but the closer we become to it, the more directly it refines us, and our lives.

Tools: Creation & Use

Tools of the Path

The Force offers us many avenues through which we can become more aligned with it. Some Forcists find that they can form and feed their connection to the Force with just their practices, and that is very true. However, it also requires an insane amount of dedication to not slip, and fail at some part of the training. There is nothing wrong with that approach, as even when we fail, we have an opportunity to learn.

However, there are several practices that can be used to help the Forcist to develop along their journey. Some are relatively common things, like various bells, meditation pillows, even the use of incense and candles. The ritualized use of spiritual clothing has already been covered, but those, too, apply. These are all tools to help us break away from our daily stresses, and grow into a more centered and spiritually powerful being. Now, even the use of these tools does not stand as insurance against failing along the Way, but they are very powerful aids in helping the student to find their way back onto their feet, once more headed up the mountain to the goal of enlightenment.

Meditation Beads

The practice of meditation beads is one almost as old as any organized religion or spiritual path. Some sects refer to them as prayer beads, others as rosary. Each application of this practice has its own unique take on what they are, how they should be made, and how they are best used. This book will not go into the various forms, and their specific meanings. Instead, we will discuss the process of creating your own set of meditation beads.

One of the most important parts of typical bead sets like this are the number of beads. I personally have three sets of meditation beads, and each represents different aspects of my development along the Ways of the Force. I have a set with medium sized round wooden beads, broken into six sets of five, with small separator beads. I made this set during my early years on the Jedi Way, and the repetition of the number five represents the five lines of the Orthodox Jedi Code, what I now teach as the Action Code. It was made during a time when I was internalizing the Code as a mantra to help me overcome emotional outbursts, such as road rage. It has no specified ends, so that it can be employed without end until calm was found.

My second set is a long, small-bead set. It is three sets of thirty-three beads, separated by three sets of five colored beads. The five bead represent the teachings of Zenryoku-kai*, a "martial life way" built specifically for the Forcist: the 5 Strengths of the Body, the 5 Illusions of the Mind, and the 5 Truths of the Force. The thirty-three natural wooden beads represent the 33 Stones of the Force, as presented earlier in this book. It is styled more like a traditional mala, with a centered point, typically called a guru bead, and a tail with a small stone In-yo charm given to me by my dear friend and apprentice, Hikaru.

The third set is a bit of a combination of the two. It still contains a guru bead, and the In-yo charm on a tail, but it is broken into three sets of eleven, separated by textured beads, whereas the thirty-three beads are smooth.

These meditation bead sets are very important to me, and very particular to my teachings of both the Force and the Jedi Way, which makes their inclusion merely examples of how they were built with intentions, and not meant to set any precedent for any Force Follower who is not of the Jedi Path, because that would be an unfair bias. Yes, they share the same Mythos, but that does not mean that they cannot be presented separately.

Now that we have looked at a few ideas of how meditation beads can be made, take the time to decide what is important to you on your Path. If I were to make a set right now, I would incorporate the seven vibration phases of the Force, but I would personally be hesitant to use the standard colors associated with the seven gateways, so as to not reinforce the separation of one phase from the other. As it is an important part on in the development of the

Forcist, I would still incorporate the 33 Stones I would also not include the guru bead, or the charm, as I find more use out of my continuous set.

But, that is just me. Each of you, put some symbolism into them, and don't be afraid to mess up. Until they are consecrated as a spiritual tool, they are just beads on some form of cord. You can take them back apart, and start over as many times as you feel like it. Give it days, weeks, even months. Decide, and then sit in meditation before making it. After you make it, sit in meditation with it again. Be sure that it is what you want it to be, and don't let yourself get locked into a belief that it has to be like one type or the other. Don't get hung up on what it is made of. Mine are inexpensive wooden beads on colored nylon cord, not polished stone beads on silk cord, or silver wire. However, do not let my draw to the humble and simple materials talk you away from the more decadent, if that is where you are being drawn. We are the subjective expression of the objective All, which means that we are part of all expressions of the Force. So long as the symbolism is sound to you, and does not stand against the values of the light of the Ashla, there is no wrong answer.

*See Appendix for more information on **Zenryoku-kai***

Focusing Talismans

Just like the meditation beads, the Forcist can create many tools to air them along the Way, called talismans. They can be an item designed to help enter a peaceful state, or to help channel the Force for a powerful working, such as Healing of self or others. In fact, the Force can manifest itself in an object to make it anything needed. A crystal used to immediately begin cleansing negative energy, a coin that helps to guide one in moments of indecision, even a wooden charm that aids in memory. The possibilities are endless, and the method of their creation is always roughly the same, although some items may take more effort than others.

First, a need must be identified. For example, something that one uses to collect kinetic energy through movement, to later be employed to help boost a healing action. Next, a proper vessel for this goal has to be chosen.

In this example, a ring would be a good choice. It is a typically minor piece of jewelry, acceptable in nearly every situation. It is also worn on the hand, which means it is always in motion whenever walking, writing, typing, or even talking. With every motion of the hand, there is kinetic energy for it to store. A plain metal band is very well suited for this application, but one that contains some crystal or stone would offer a better point of storage, and focus for output when releasing the energy.

Now that the need has been identified, and the vessel has been chosen, we begin the programming of the talisman.

We first begin with the skills learned through the psychometry practices listed earlier. We dive in, and read the history of the object. From there, we have to decide if the history is of benefit to the new goal, or if it will interfere. For example, if looking to build a talisman for healing, something that has a violent history is not the best choice. That does not mean that you cannot use the item, only that it should be energetically cleansed first.

Once you have a solid reading of the item's history, you can pull away at part of it, or all of it. That skill is a bit different for everyone, so just experiment with the process. Some see the parts just fall off and disappear, some see them fade into a wisp of smoke. Others still watch them burn, or wipe them away with their hands, flicking off the negative energy like touching something damp. Repeat this process several times to be sure that you have removed all echoes of the past from the item, leaving it clear of any negative energy imprints.

After this, you will begin to focus on the exact nature of what you need this talisman to do. Don't imagine it, feel it. Manifest this programming into the item. Do so without doubt, but do it slowly and thoroughly. Pour energy into the item for as long as you can hold the feeling. Once your focus begins to waiver, it is important that you stop immediately, so as to not instill some flaw in the structure you are building in the item. Repeat this charging and programming step as many times as needed until the intention takes life, like the birth of a small star, stable and powerful.

Programming a talisman like this can be a simple practice, but it can be of amazing benefit for the practice of the Ways of the Force. As with any skill, repetition leads to proficiency, but along that same thread, do not beat yourself up if it takes you several days to properly create your first talisman. The Force comes to each of us in very unique, and specific ways, and you may have little skill in this practice, or you may have a great potential for it. Just know yourself, and trust in the Force, and you will succeed.

Forcist Staff

The use of a staff in the Forcist practices was touched on earlier, but this is the process of making your own staff, rather than simply using something produced by the hands of another. Much like the practice of creating meditation beads, this step is amazingly personal, but it is also a rite of passage for the Forcist. It is through this process that the student begins to build their own manifestation within the Force. It is through this that the Forcist becomes more than just a student of the Path, but begins to take their first steps into the holistic nature of the Way.

This process is important, and as such should never be rushed. This should not be something that is done, start to finish, in a weekend. It should take weeks, or even months, to complete the Forcist staff. That is because the first part of this is to know who you are, and how you are one with the Force. What type of

Forcist are you going to be? Are you a Guardian, ready to step into harm's way should you be called to do so? Are you a Monk, dedicated to the spiritual refinement of the self over all else? Are you the Mystic, who focuses on making their impact on the world through the limitlessness of the Force over any physical acts? Are you any mixture of the three? Are you something else, like a Healer, or a Seer? The Force does not shoehorn us into such limited roles, so don't expect to fit any of them totally. Just be aware that your Path should be represented in your staff, so that it can act as an ever-present reminder of who you are, and what you are striving to become.

These points are important in planning the creation of the staff. For example, weaving together three vines to harden into an intricate pattern is a fabulous endeavor for the Monk, as it draws on patience, but it would be a poor choice for the Guardian who may need to defend himself or others with his staff, as it would break more easily. A fresh, green limb can be dried and hardened, smoothed, and wrapped in leather or cord, which is ideal for the Guardian, but may hinder the connection to life called for by the Mystic. A deep, exotic wood can be wrapped in metal and stones, and adorned with feathers found on the Mystic's walks in nature, but could prove too ornate for the simple goals of the Monk.

Once you have seen where on the Path that your feet rest, you can now begin the process of educating yourself on the various options of wood available. Should you plan to train with the staff as a self-defense aid, you should focus on hardwoods that can stand up to the rigors of training over a lifetime, no matter if Guardian or otherwise. Through the power of the internet, any wood imaginable can be acquired as a starting point, but I always recommend that the Forcist go out into nature, and let the staff come to them. This can be a long process, but the Ways of the Force have no end on this plane, so there is time.

Look for trees felled through acts of nature, such as a storm or heavy ice. Walk through the woods, and look for stout limbs, or trunks of smaller trees. In time, the Force will bring you to directly where you are supposed to be to find our staff. Once you find the proper limb, shave it down into a straight dowel, keeping a thickness that fills your hand comfortably without being too thin. After this, research the best ways to allow the wood you are using to naturally dry, so as to not damage the wood in the next step.

Once you have the blank dowel, it is time to adorn the staff as you see fit. Remember, this staff is a representation of who you are, and where you are going. If you are striving to leave behind a habit of materialism, ornate decoration and vivid hues would not be the best choice. If you are coming away from
a past that has taken a toll on your body, keeping the right height and sturdiness would be more important than anything. Should you aim for the higher workings of the Force, perhaps runes or sigils should be carved into the shaft, making sure to not ruin the strength of the staff in the process. Be mindful in this

process, and once more, do not rush it. No part of this should be finished in a single day's time. Be sure that you actually want the changes you are about to make, and then be very intentional and careful in making these modifications to avoid mistakes or regrets later.

Once the staff has been formed and forged to your liking, and intention, we must bond with it, and become one with the Force in it, and awaken the wood. First, we will once more use psychometry to strip away all of the past of the staff. Even if you harvest your own limb, and hand carve it into shape, that is still an extension of your intention onto and into the wood. We have to remove that as completely as possible. Perform this cleansing at least three times, but if a mass-produced dowel is chosen, then seven cleansing sessions are recommended. Wood is an organic material, and actually holds onto imprints more than things like metal. The Force in the staff must be as pure as possible, because our next step is to bring life back to the wood.

This process can take some time, so be sure that you are not in any hurry, or under any time constraints. You can embellish the following ritual, making it a more grand experience. There is merit to such trappings as ceremonial robes, candles, incense, and the like. It helps to put us into a more altered state, where we can better shut out the troubles of the world, and be more open to the Force. However, that is not required. All that is required is that you be able to enter a meditative state, and direct the Force.

Place the staff in front of you, be it on a table, or the ground. Lower your head, as you enter the meditative state by following the In Out method taught at the beginning of the chapter on Meditation. Once you are centered, feel the Force in your body as a vibrant light. See in your mind's eye this light getting denser at your hands. Place your hands close together, and feel the flow of the energy out one hand, and in the other.

Next, you are going to pick up the staff by the

ends, but be mindful of the flow of energy in your hands. *If using the staff as a Forcework aid, be sure that the hand that is projecting energy grabs the bottom of the staff, and the hand that draws in energy is at the top of the staff.* This is important, as the process will help to build an energy channel in the wood, and a Forcework casting staff needs to have a channel that casts up and out, rather than down.

Fill the staff, from end to end, with the Force in the form of the vibrant light, as it pours from your hands. Allow it to flow from end to end, gradually holding the energy as the flow continues. In time, the staff will glow as vibrantly as the Force in your body. From this point, increase the intensity of the Force as it flows into you, and through the staff. Push more and more, until it feels like your body is going to collapse, and the staff is going to break. Once you can push any harder, drop the staff on the ground or table, and decrease your personal flow.

Doing this is the process of returning the living energy of the Force to the once-living tree, and thus awakening the nature spirit within it. It may take more than one charging session, but when you are done, you will be able to feel the shift in the presence of the staff. It will have a gravity, possibly a pulse like a heartbeat, or breathing. You will feel yourself in the staff, but that sense of you will begin to change, as it intermingles with the echo of the tree.

This is called an awakened tool. It has a point of your soul in it, bound with the soul of the life it was before. It will act as a conduit to the natural world around you, and give better connection to the Force in any area where you hold it. This process can be done with other objects, such as blades, but the more processed the material, the further it is from its natural state. That makes metal of any refined state less directly connected, but still a viable option. Plastics and other processed polymers are nearly impossible, because it is what is called a spiritually dead material. While the Forcist is not one who holds a bias against modern technology, it does pose some challenges when it comes to some Forcework.

The Culmination

An End, and a Beginning

This brings us to a very important part of one's training: free exploration. This book is designed to offer a quick, but concise overview of the teachings and practices of the Forcist, and act as a bridge between the Force and other traditions. However, it is not the Book of All Things. As such, all Forcists must take the journey into the adjacent worlds around them, and learn to be more. Expand on who you are, and what it means to you to be a student of the Ways of the Force.

A Forcist is a wide variety of a great many things: warrior, mystic, monk, healer and seer. However, what we are most are seekers of knowledge, questing for understanding and direction. That is what put this book in your hand, and what has driven you to read it, in part or in whole. You are driven by the Force to become more aware of what is around you, seen and unseen, known and unknown. Do not think that, just because there is a ton of information presented here, that it is anywhere near much more than scratching the surface. So, go! Go out into the world, and learn more. Learn deeper! Question the world around you, and even continue to question the answers that you find. However, do not lose yourself in the process. Sometimes there is not a good answer, or any answer at all. Make mistakes, because that is the only way that we really learn. Remember, the master fails more times than the mere student ever tries.

The master also grows in their Path, and lives their Way. They have transcended the line between being a Forcist, a statement of action, and being Forcist, a statement of living. Once you learn what you can, both from this book and any other sources you may encounter, do not hold too tightly to any one interpretation.

That locks us into the Guru mind, and can blind us to deeper and more complete understanding.

Live simply, give generously, aid fearlessly, and learn endlessly.

The Force calls us to do one thing above all else, and that is to make the world better, to help bring the balance of the Ashla to the world around us. We have been gifted the method and understanding to impact the world in a way that few other Paths can, because we are part of the spiritual revolution of the here and now. We have brought with us the wisdom of the past masters, and placed it in the forefront for everyone to see, and benefit from.

So, go into the world, and leave it a better place, even if just a little each day. Just as a dripping of water can erode stone, so too can small acts of goodness turn the tide of the world. If you feel that you must be open about your spiritual path, do as you feel you must, but do not ever think that you are obligated to do so. Guide people to goodness through action, not merely speaking of good things.

Let our good actions be for what we are known. If you are meant to spread the word, the Force will be sure to bring to you the right set of ears. If that happens, pass on what you have learned, and let the Ways of the Force grow with you.

Surely, some of you will come to this book without any knowledge or connection to the online Jedi community, and will want to know more about it, because of the direct connection of terminology and mythos. That is your right and choice, but I want to reinforce the need to wander, to quest, to grow. Do not just go to one source, and take their actions as gospel, because there are many people walking these spiritual journeys, and we are all just as lost as anyone else. Keep your eyes open, and be sure to see things as they are. Also, especially if looking at any spiritual or esoteric groups online, remember that some people are going to be hung up on certain things in their own journey, and it can make them be pretty unwelcoming, even potentially hostile. Just know that the Force will get them through it, if they can quiet their screaming pain and hear that guiding whisper in the quiet part of their soul.

This is important in our dealings with all people. We are each a subjective expression of the objective All. In that, we are all a part of the Force, and together, we are one in and with the Force. So, be sure to keep the correct mind when dealing with others. When faced with oppression of any kind, we must be willing to step in harm's way, and stand up for those downtrodden, but still show what compassion can be afforded. Know that justice tempered with compassion is the best way that we can restore the harmonious balance of the Ashla, and that we are called to keep that balance.

Know that there is still goodness in everyone, and so long as they take breath, there is some flash of the divine spark of the All. That spark, that pure core of the Force in each person is what we seek to find, and nurture, in ourselves and others, so we must keep that in mind when dealing with difficult, or toxic people. That can be hard, because toxicity often echoes out into the Force around others.

Appendix

Terminology to Remember

Akashic Record: see *Astral Temple*
Ashla: harmonious balance, often referred to as the Light.
Astral Temple: depository of all knowledge, found in the Cosmic frequency of the Force.
Bogan: malicious imbalance, often referred to as the Dark.
Chakra: see *Gateway*
Forceform: the energetic body, also referred to as the astral body.
Forcework: all forms of direct manipulations of the Force, be it free form or ritualized
Forcist: Force follower, student of the spiritual and mystical Ways of the Force
Gateway: energy center in the human body, mostly centralized along the spinal column, but also found in the palms of the hands, and soles of the feet.
In-yo: an older Japanese symbol that shows the shifting nature of the dynamic balance, similar to Chinese concept of *yin yang*

Jedi: sub-sect of Force follower, held to the Code and Philosophy of the marital knights, as presented in the mythos.

Mythos: the *Star Wars* media from which the framework of the Ways of the Force were structured, as well as the source of many lessons for the Forcist.

Outside Resources

Looking Within: A Guide on Meditation
Justin Gates & Charles McBride Jr.
Knights of Awakening, Nov 2020
ISBN-13: 979-8556221673

One of the most complete looks at meditation as an ancient and modern practice. This books not only delves into the what and how of meditation, but also the why. A collaborative effort by the Knights of Awakening, this book is a must for any Forcist, Neopagan, or modern Occultist.

A collaborative effort from the greater Force Follower Community, as well as parallel groups, this book does a fantastic job at presenting the ancient practice in a way that makes it more relevant and accessible to the modern pathwalker of any level of experience.

Zenryoku-kai: Jedi Combat Arts
http://jediarts.site

The mythos beneath the Way of the Force, and of the online Jedi movement is filled with references to the practice of the martial arts. As the longest-active member of the online Jedi Community and life-long martial artist, Otori Mikko has begun the on-going development of Zenryoku-kai, the Jedi Combat Arts (JCA).

What began as an attempt at creating a single martial practice for the entire online Jedi Community, the Staff Short Form, has evolved to include the Breathwork Exercises, as well as the Hand Form and the Short Stick Form. Zenryoku-kai is still growing, and being refined, bringing in other martial arts experts from within the greater Force Follower Community, to create a more complete, multi-faceted system for the training and betterment of all members who train in it.

Jedi Seeker YouTube Channels
http://youtube.com/@jediseeker
http://youtube.com/@jedipathworking

There are many great resources for those wishing to learn more about the Force, and the Life Path most directly connected to it, the Jedi. These channels are part of the *Jedi Seekers Network*, and are highly recommended for anyone wanting to learn a bit more about the depths of the Way.